The *Art* of
Teaching the *Bible*

The *Art* of *Teaching* the *Bible*

A PRACTICAL GUIDE FOR ADULTS

Christine Eaton Blair

Geneva Press
Louisville, Kentucky

Scripture quotations from the New Revised Standard Version of the Bible are copyright © 1989 by the Division of Christian Education of the National Council of the Churches of Christ in the U.S.A. and are used by permission.

Excerpt from *Rachel the Clever and Other Jewish Folktales* by Josepha Sherman. Copyright 1993 by Josepha Sherman. Used by permission of August House Publishers, Inc.

Excerpt reprinted from *Stories for the Journey* by William R. White. Copyright 1988 Augsburg Publishing House. Used by permission of Augsburg Fortress.

Book design by Sharon Adams
Cover design by Arisman Design, Essex, MA

First Edition
Published by Geneva Press
Louisville, Kentucky

This book is printed on acid-free paper that meets the American National Standards Institute Z39.48 standard. ⊗

PRINTED IN THE UNITED STATES OF AMERICA

01 02 03 04 05 06 07 08 09 10 — 10 9 8 7 6 5 4 3 2 1

Library of Congress Cataloging-in-Publication Data

Blair, Christine Eaton, 1949–
    The art of teaching the Bible : a practical guide for adults / Christine Eaton Blair.—1st ed.
        p. cm.
    Includes bibliographical references and index.
    ISBN 0-664-50148-6 (alk. paper)
    1. Bible—Study and teaching. I. Title.

BS600.3 .B53 2001
220'.071'5—dc21   00-047675

*To my parents
who modeled the art of teaching to me
and to my husband, Marvin Steinmetz,
and our daughter, Gillian—
their love brings beauty to the canvas of my life*

Contents

Preface

I have always loved a good Bible study. In the early 1970s, while I was living at the American Church in Paris, France, Dr. Robert Jewett, a New Testament scholar in residence there, led stimulating Bible studies. He personally persuaded me to go study the original languages. The next year I attended the American Baptist Seminary of the West in Berkeley to study in the area of religious education. In the late 1970s, a weekend retreat for Presbyterian lay leaders, led by biblical scholar Dr. James A. Sanders, precipitated me back to seminary in Claremont, California. There I eventually earned a Ph.D. in religious education with a dissertation about teaching liberating Bible study to women.

In seminary, and later as a pastor, I was haunted by the question of why Protestant laity seem so ill acquainted and ill at ease with the Bible. I wondered how I and other church leaders could be more effective in our teaching. I taught youth and adult Bible studies, and I trained others to lead such studies. I was supported in my search most strongly by the Presbyterian Women's groups of my churches in California: First Presbyterian Church of Oxnard and Claremont Presbyterian Church. I give them my love and my gratitude for their affirmation of my questions, my teaching, and my pastoring and for all that they taught me. I was accepted and encouraged in this quest, and in all my work with the Presbyterian Church (U.S.A.) by the Rev. Dr. Bear Ride, my colleague in ministry for many years and my dear friend.

When I moved to Texas, many church leaders in the Synod of the Sun pressed me with more questions about teaching the Bible to adults, questions about methods, tools, activities, and content. I was invited to teach presbytery- and synod-level workshops on this subject; these experiences allowed me to listen to a broad spectrum of church leaders and their concerns. This book grows out of these workshops and the research they galvanized me to do. The work I did was fueled by my love of teaching and my love of the Bible. (It should be noted that portions of the material in chapter 2 first appeared in a modified version in *Theological Education* 34, no. 1 [Autumn 1997].)

I am grateful for all the help and support I received on this project. The enthusiasm and keen insights of my editor, Carey C. Newman, encouraged me and guided me in just the way an adult likes to be guided. Jennifer Everett, my assistant at Austin Seminary, played happily with my grammar and my format; I thank her especially for work on details that eluded me. I owe a debt of gratitude to Austin Presbyterian Theological Seminary for providing me with generous sabbatical time for research and writing and with good friends and colleagues who have helped me mature in my thinking and teaching. Most important, the unwavering love and insightful questions of my pastor husband, Marvin Steinmetz, and the joy of learning and love of our small daughter, Gillian, have made all this possible and worthwhile.

Introduction

At an ecumenical meeting of Christian educators and pastors, the topic of teaching the Bible comes up. One educator sketches out the problem as she sees it:

"At the heart of the Protestant tradition is the understanding that every person has the right and the duty to read the Bible, which is God's Word to us. But few people in my Methodist congregation these days seem to know much about the Bible. When I ask them to open the pew Bible and read along with me, they are lost. And when we offer Bible study classes, they don't come!"

Another educator jumps in:

"We Baptists are known for being Bible-centered, but my people don't really know the Bible well either. We offer all sorts of Bible study classes for our adults, but they don't sign up. My teachers are frustrated too. They think the problem is that Bible study is boring for the adults. Teachers are unsure about how to present the material in a way that is appealing to adults. They can't get class members to read and study during the week. And in class, they sometimes have a hard problem getting a good discussion going."

A pastor joins the discussion.

"I have some of those same problems in my Presbyterian

1

congregation—like the Methodists, many of them don't know the Bible, and like the Baptists, teachers are frustrated about how to motivate and interest the adults. But I think the problem goes even further: We haven't taught our adults how to interpret the biblical texts. They get confused when different Bible passages seem to contradict each other. When they have a problem, they simply try to apply a favorite Bible verse in some sort of literal or wooden fashion.

"They don't understand the gaps between their world and the biblical world. They are intimidated by scholarly experts—even by me, their pastor—when we talk about the Greek and the Hebrew meanings of words or about the social norms of those cultures and times. And when they hear some people on radio and TV, they often know that they disagree, but they don't know why."

The church leaders continue to bat around the problem of adult Bible study. They wonder about the large, in-depth Bible studies like Disciple, Kerygma, *and* Bethel. *Some of them point out that these curricula require training and money, and their churches have neither money nor people who have time for the training. One adds the problem of figuring what whether a study is good or not: "How can I look through published Bible studies and make a judgment about whether it will teach what we want and need in an interesting manner?" "I know," replies another, "I often create my own Bible study and so do my teachers. I wish I'd had more training on how to do this well."*

This scenario presents questions that are typical in churches today. Four major problems are presented by our imaginary educators and pastors:

- Adult biblical illiteracy—How do we motivate and educate adults to know the Bible?
- Teaching methods—How can we teach adults effectively?

- Interpretation—How can adults learn to use modern tools and theological principles to interpret the biblical texts for themselves?
- Curriculum—How do we evaluate and get access to what's "good"?

Church leaders are frustrated about how to teach the Bible. They strongly believe that the study of the Bible is at the heart of the Christian faith. It is "the Word of the Lord" for us Christians and provides the "rule of faith and life."[1] Through the Bible, we hear God's call to us. We learn of God's story and the story of the people through whom God has worked. Most important for Christians, through the Bible we come to understand the great gift given to us in Jesus Christ. We encounter the depth of God's grace and love for us. And we are instructed in how we should live, in response to this great love. How can our people, we wonder, live as faithful Christians if they do not know the Bible?

This book aims to address problems that I have heard about frequently from Christian educators, such as those problems described above. The overall thesis of this book is that teaching Bible study is an art necessitating certain methods and skills that grow out of understanding the two interacting texts: *the biblical text* and *the text formed by the lives of the adults*. The art of teaching does more than simply guide the reading and discussion of biblical passages. The artist/teacher recognizes that the Bible and the learners need to connect in a meaningful manner. This connection requires understanding the nature of the biblical texts, their history and shape, and the ways in which they have been interpreted. It also requires understanding adult learners: how they learn and what their life contexts are demanding of them.

Through knowledge of the Bible and adult learners, teaching methods and tools can be developed to make the teacher more skillful and effective. Just as a painter must be taught the medium of paint and canvas and must develop ease with tools such as brushes and palette, so too teachers need help in developing their knowledge and skills. The artist/teacher uses her skill to help create a teaching-learning canvas that guides adult students to find connections between the scriptures and their lives, connections that will enable them to live more faithfully as disciples of Jesus Christ. This teaching process becomes an art as it evolves beyond skills, growing out of the teacher's love for the Bible and her learners, and enlivened by the inspiration of God's Spirit.

The teacher as artist is not using the students as a blank canvas upon which he places color and texture. Instead, he guides the learners to become beginning artists, exploring and interpreting the texts of the Bible and their lives through the teaching-learning process. He also learns along with them. This *process* is as important as the final product in this art, for making connections between Bible and life never comes to a complete stop, and the skills learned by the students can continue to be used long after formal study has ended. To direct this process, the artist/teacher needs to develop knowledge of both the Bible and the learners and to develop teaching skills that, like good color and brushwork, enhance learning.

To guide the teacher in this endeavor, the first chapter explores different understandings that are brought by Christians to the interpretation of the Bible. These differences put a unique shape on educational goals and process, even though each individual understands the Bible to be the Word of God and Holy Scripture. These goals of Bible study grow out of interpretive differences and help guide the artist/teacher in determining which educational methods will be used. An understanding of interpretive differences also begins to address the question of adequate interpretation and appropriate curriculum.

Too often, the concern in teaching the Bible is only with the Bible and with how to transfer biblical texts into the (blank) mind of the students. Good teaching, however, values the adults. For the teacher using God the Master Artist as model, each individual is a child of God, loved and valued by God. Therefore chapter 2 brings to the artist/teacher a detailed summary of current research in adult learning. This summary is set in a format that I hope will be useful for training other teachers, called "Adults Learn Best When . . ." Understanding adult learning and teaching helps the teacher understand how to motivate and interest adults.

Based upon the ways in which adults learn best, and a summary of different ways scripture is understood, a model for teaching is proposed in chapter 3 that teachers and pastors have found useful. This is the "five Rs model" (remembering, revisiting the text, reflecting critically, reinterpreting, and responding). Just as an artist must be taught a variety of ways to use the brush with the paint and canvas, this model offers teachers a variety of techniques to teach adults within an overall step-by-step framework. Together the five Rs allow for the learners to listen carefully to the Bible and to connect it to their lives and their community. It builds in a variety of educational methods and activities so that different styles of learning can be modeled and different modes of listening to and interpreting the text can be experienced. The five Rs help guide teachers who wish to create a richly textured and faithful study.

The five Rs model is not, however, the only one that can be used. For the artist/teacher who prefers to create her own plan or to use a printed curriculum, chapter 4 describes three basic educational elements that need to be intermixed for sound adult Bible study. These are called the "three primary colors" of Bible study. Just as red, blue, and yellow are blended to form many colors and shades of a painting, so can these three educational ingredients be intermixed: analytical reflection, storytelling and disciplined imagination, and action through ritual and ministry. Whereas in chapter 3 these "colors" are blended in the five Rs model, in chapter 4 the teacher can study the theory behind these colors and use them to evaluate printed Bible study curriculum or for developing her own model.

Taking on the task of teaching the Bible is a challenge in today's world. Teaching takes training and practice, and over time, as skills and knowledge are put to use, it becomes easier. Chapter 5 consists of ten teaching tips that I have found helpful. My hope is that it will encourage all teachers, novices and masters, to reflect on the craft of teaching. Then, as we perfect our craft and grow in our love for the Bible and our learners, we may receive the gift of the Holy Spirit to move into that indefinable mode we call "art." To be an artist is to have moments of inspiration and of joy. It is this that I wish for every teacher of the Bible.

Chapter One

Educational Goals and Biblical Interpretation: Four Models

> With my whole heart I seek you;
> do not let me stray from your commandments.
> I treasure your word in my heart,
> so that I may not sin against you. . . .
> I will delight in your statutes;
> I will not forget your word.
>
> Psalm 119:10–11, 16

The central written text in Bible study is the Bible. The artist/teacher needs to think carefully about the nature of this text and about the ways in which it is used and interpreted in contemporary communities of faith. Our mission as Bible study teachers is to help adults listen to the biblical texts and make connections with their own lives. To be skillful teachers, we must deepen our understanding of this text. In this chapter we explore a variety of ways in which the Bible is understood and interpreted by different Christian groups. Given these variations, we can identify different educational goals and questions, and we can name our own interpretive biases; for an important step in being an artist is being self-aware.

Our goals in teaching the Bible are determined in large part by our understanding of what the Bible is.

For most Christians, the Bible is the Word of God. It is scripture, that is, sacred writings that convey knowledge of God. While God's ultimate revelation is in flesh, in Jesus Christ, the Bible is also God's revelation to us.

Yet the ways in which we understand God's revelation differ in our various traditions. The Bible contains a wide variety of symbols, images, and stories. In every Christian group, certain symbols and stories become more central than others. Certain ideas become dominant over others. As a result, scripture as "Word" conveys a variety of images and understandings.[1]

Viewing the Bible differently leads to different educational goals. For example, if we see the Bible as the Word of a transcendent God, our goal will be to help people to know and memorize the stories and verses.[2] If, however, we understand the Bible as the story of the people of God, our goal will be to help our parishioners to hear and understand this story and to make connections with their own story.[3] Although these two ways of understanding the Bible are not necessarily exclusive, they do result in different teaching goals.

Religious educators have long wrestled with the issue of goals for teaching the Bible. I have sorted their thoughts into different models, grouping together the educational goal and the central vision of what the Bible is (see chart on p. 23). It is important to note that, for each model, the authority of the Bible is not in question. For each group the Bible is authoritative, revelatory of God and of Jesus Christ. The differences are differences of interpretation and vision.

Conversion

The Bible as Encounter
of the Holy God with Sinful Humanity

> Have mercy on me, O God,
> according to your steadfast love;
> according to your abundant mercy
> blot out my transgressions.
> Wash me thoroughly from my iniquity,
> and cleanse me from my sin.
> > Psalm 51:1–2

The central image in this concept of the Bible is that of holy God—sinful humanity. As a result, the goal of teaching the Bible is for the reader to be confronted with "the mind and spirit of Christ." It is the goal of *conversion* of both the individual and the church. The goal of conversion helps the learner explore the key question: *In what ways do I need to repent and have my life, and the life of the church and the world, transformed by the holy God?*

For educators with this goal, "the ultimate and disastrous illusion" we humans can have is "the identification of anything in [ourselves] with God."[4] Humans are alien from God. Meaning is given to human life from beyond, by a God who is present in history and yet is external, hidden, different, and holy. God's involvement confronts humans with their blindness, their need for judgment and new life, their sinfulness.

God's ways are visible only to the eyes of faith, an awakening that comes through encountering the

Bible. The hidden, mysterious, and transcendent God has been revealed through the experiences of Israel and then through Jesus Christ, but can only be known by each new generation through the scriptures.[5]

Although composed of many different writings, the Bible is "the self-disclosure of God."[6] While for some believers, each word and phrase has been divinely inspired, most "mainline" church leaders understand that biblical writings are human words that convey the "Word of God."[7] The Bible contains a unity of witness to the God who confronts, calls, and responds to humans. The authors of the Bible "stand firmly with God in the unseen and from there look penetratingly into our human situation."[8] The assumption is that the Bible starts from the holy God and works down to sinful humankind.

The confrontation through the Bible with the holy God also renews and reconverts the church, liberating it from paralyzing ideas and structures. To be so converted, the church needs the tie with its community of origin as represented in scripture. Such faithful existence must be true to its roots and at the same time contemporary in its message and witness to God today. Through the Bible, Christians are called to live in two worlds, one ancient and one modern, and to find the realities of God's presence in both. The very alienness of the biblical texts can be helpful for underlining the "otherness" of God.[9]

In order to be converted by the holy God, we need to be taught to memorize and probe the biblical text. We can learn to use the results of biblical scholarship to understand the meaning of the text in the past and to make this text part of our own world. Through the scriptures, we are challenged to answer God's call.

To encounter the holy God, study of the Bible

must be carried out only in the context of the community of faith. The community of faith, as well as the Bible, is the dwelling place of the risen Christ and can confront sinful humanity. Both the Bible and the community of faith, therefore, are necessary parts of conversation that reveals God's presence. The emphasis in this educational approach, however, is on scripture confronting the community of faith, rather than the community of faith confronting scripture.

The strength of this model lies in its strong understanding of the holiness, sovereignty, and freedom of God. In a world often unaware of the mystery of the transcendent, this call to conversion awakens us to the need each one of us has for the Holy in our lives. This model also reminds us of God's call to us as the church to be faithful. Through the Bible, read with a common-sense approach, God will convert each of us and send us out to change our communities and nations.

The weakness of this model lies in its strength: by emphasizing the large gap between humans and God, it can make God seem inapproachable and unloving. Interpreting Holy Scripture can seem even more difficult, if not impossible, and thus alienating to learners. In a world wracked with pain and in a culture of positivism, this model can be difficult to communicate.

In sum, the image of the Bible as divine self-revelation places an emphasis on the holiness of God and the sinfulness of humans. The Bible thus plays the role of confronting humans with God's judgment and grace in Jesus Christ. The goal of teaching the Bible is to confront us with a holy God, known in Jesus Christ, and to convert us out of sin into a new and holy way. This educational goal is accomplished by an interpretation of the Bible that stresses the faithfulness and holiness of God throughout the history of human unfaithfulness and sin.

The goal of conversion helps the learner explore the key question: *In what ways do I need to repent and have my life, and the life of the church and the world, transformed by the holy God?* This model can lead to an educational emphasis on memorization and analysis of texts and of the doctrines revealed by these texts.

Common Identity with Bible People

God's Story Told through Community Stories

> Hear, O Israel: The LORD is our God, the LORD alone. . . . Keep these words that I am commanding you today in your heart. Recite them to your children and talk about them when you are at home and when you are away, when you lie down and when you rise.
>
> Deuteronomy 6:4, 6–7

Over the centuries the communities of faith interpreted and reinterpreted the biblical tradition, adding story and song to emphasize one strand of tradition or to negate another strand. In each generation the story of God was retold in a way that responded to the particular questions and problems of that generation. In each generation the story brought life and identity by answering the questions "Who are we?" and "What are we to do?"[10] In time, the stories and their interpretations were woven together to become scripture, the Bible, our sacred texts. Sacred texts are those that function as authoritative, life-giving text for the believing community.[11]

The educational goal, then, is to identify ourselves with the biblical communities of the past, in order to link ourselves to God's story. The key educational question in this model is centered on the biblical believing communities and their stories: *How do the biblical stories of the past and our stories today reveal the one God at work?*

Believers rooted in this understanding of the Bible have a rich awareness of the Holy Spirit at work in the lives of believing communities, past and present. Whereas the previous model stresses the sinfulness of humans, this model stresses the ways communities and individuals, even in their sin, were able to be guided by the Holy Spirit to do God's work. God's faithfulness and humanity's openness to the Spirit (if only a partial openness) have in the past overcome sin and serve as scriptural guides to us in the present day.

For those believers with these understandings, the Bible by itself is not the Word of God. The Word of God is the meeting of the biblical text with the community, whether in the past or the present.[12] The presence of the Holy Spirit in the formation of the Bible and in the gatherings of the faithful makes the Bible a living, dynamic Word.

Educators in this model are thus interested in the ways in which the tradition was reinterpreted each generation. By identifying the methods of interpretation used by the biblical writers, we will be helped in interpreting the Bible in our context today. In this manner we can identify with the faithful communities of the past described in the Bible and connect our story to God's story. This connection may then help us to experience a fundamental shift in the way that we see life, its problems, and its solutions.[13]

If the Bible has many different kinds of writings, with no one unifying theme or concept, if it is the stories of many past communities, where is its unity? The unity of the Bible is found in who God is; it is the monotheistic emphasis placed on the One, centered in the Shema from Deuteronomy: "Hear (*Shema*), O Israel: The LORD is our God, the LORD alone" (Deut. 6:4). Each generation in the Bible wrestled with ways to pull back from the worship of idols or of "powers and principalities" to the one God, the God of judgment and mercy. In other words, whereas the previous model emphasized doctrine and judgment, this model stresses God's Story of faithfulness.

The interpretations and stories employed by the biblical communities give God's Story life and meaning in each new generation; in a variety of ways they call the people back to monotheism. The biblical stories provide models for us today, models of how to interpret God's Story in our own time. An example is the Exodus story, which took on new meaning and gave new shape to the worship life of the Israelites every time a major national catastrophe arose. The Bible thus provides many ways to carry on the tradition, a rich pluralism that makes the Bible a living document. No one set of actions works in every generation. The Bible as a model, rather than as a set of doctrines, thereby remains a source of life and salvation for every generation.[14]

The goal of teaching the Bible, then, is to help readers identify themselves with the biblical communities of faith and to link our stories with the one God's Story.[15] Studying the Bible can illuminate both our faithfulness and our unfaithfulness. It is study that can be comforting yet challenging, urging us away from the idols and delusions of our polytheistic lives.

This method has several strengths. God is more accessible and imminent. The emphasis on the very human biblical witnesses to God's Story makes reading the Bible less intimidating. The stories of God's work, even through weak and unfaithful people, give today's world hope. The predominance of stories, furthermore, encourages creative and involving educational processes.

Weaknesses in this model come when learners identify too easily with the faithful and overlook the need for their own repentance and ongoing conversion. The steadfast presence of God can sometimes be assumed too quickly by learners, who thereby lose the sense of mystery and awe of the love of the Holy One. An overly glib assumption of faithfulness could lead believers to forget the need for God's work and God's grace.

In sum, this model's emphasis is on the faithful communities' witness rather than on the holy God. Humanity is seen as both faithful and sinful. Its key question, *How do the biblical stories of the past and our stories today reveal the one God at work?* begins with human experience, past and present, and moves to God (and then back to humans). This model leads to education that emphasizes stories: stories of biblical peoples and stories of today's peoples.

Justice/Faith in Action

God's Call for Social Transformation and Shalom

The Spirit of the Lord is upon me,
because he has anointed me
to bring good news to the poor.
He has sent me to proclaim release to the captives,
and recovery of sight to the blind,

to let the oppressed go free,
to proclaim the year of the Lord's favor.

Luke 4:18–19

Early in this century, a religious educator described the Bible as a "great body of symbols" in which God reveals that we are called to radical love of our neighbor. It is in this love of neighbor, lived out through social justice, that we show our love for God. The goal of teaching the Bible is not simply to instill knowledge and power but to teach the right use of knowledge in power and to transform society.[16]

The goal of teaching the Bible for this educator, and for others like him in more recent times, is to help us see the injustices within contemporary society and to inspire us to work as God's partners to transform society and bring about God's kingdom. The Bible helps us to critique the current social realities in light of the deeper realities and demands of God revealed in the Bible.

The key question grows out of this model: *What work are we called to do as a community acting in Jesus' name to "proclaim good news to the poor" and "freedom to the captive"?* The educational emphasis is on living out our Christian faith in faithful action. For some learners, study of the Bible begins with action—building a house for the homeless, serving in a downtown soup kitchen and shelter, and so forth—and then linking their experience and stories with the call for justice by the biblical, righteous God.

This model has gained prominence in recent times, especially in countries and communities where violence, oppression, and poverty predominate. Educators and church leaders have concluded that a key image in the Bible is that of the righteous God of justice and freedom, the God who cares deeply about the poor, abused, and downtrodden of society.[17] The words of the prophets, the words of Jesus in his parable of judgment (Matt. 25:30ff.), and the lifestyle of the early Christians pictured in Acts all contribute to this image as a key metaphor. The Exodus story, a story of God's liberation of a rabble of slaves who become a chosen people, is repeated throughout the Bible and therefore is seen as the central story, the model for our story as Christians.[18] As liberated people, we work as God's partners to bring about God's kingdom and God's peace, revealed in flesh in Jesus Christ.[19]

Paired with the call for justice and liberation is an element of suspicion. Suspicion is brought to bear on past interpretations of biblical texts that helped to promote injustices, such as justifying the poverty of the poor or the silencing of women. Past and present interpretations, and even biblical texts themselves, are examined for their faithfulness in representing God as liberator of the poor and oppressed. The impact of these interpretations on society is also carefully studied.[20]

The strength of this model is the emphasis on social analysis and action for justice. This understanding of the Bible demands changes in how we live out our faith. It asks believers to see the world as God does, with extra love and concern for the poor and oppressed. It therefore shows learners how to link study and faith, church and society. It often necessitates an experiential method of teaching and learning, such as a praxis method. This method, which interacts action and reflection, is very helpful to many contemporary adults, who become impatient with "abstract" study.

The weakness of this model lies in the stress on one image to the possible exclusion of others. With the emphasis on our work as God's partners in the transformation of society, God's sovereignty and grace can be forgotten. People can begin to believe that it is all up to them and become discouraged and tired. In addition, the emphasis on societal transformation, while very necessary, may hide the necessity for personal conversion and transformation.

In sum, this model centers in the image of the righteous God of justice and freedom who calls the faithful to action on behalf of the poor and powerless. The educational goal, then, is to help believers see the needs of this world and to challenge them to act as God's partners in transformation. The key question for the learner is this: *What work are we called to do as a community acting in Jesus' name to "proclaim good news to the poor" and "freedom to the captive"?* Educational methods, as a result, include analysis of contemporary society and personal experience, coupled with actions that work for justice and peace, based in biblical understandings.

Spiritual Growth into a Holy Life

God's Faithful Love

> As a deer longs for flowing streams,
> so my soul longs for you, O God.
> Psalm 42:1

Verses such as this capture the longing of individuals to grow closer to the loving God, through knowledge of God and personal development of sanctity. Individuals often see the Bible as the inspiration for personal spiritual development and private piety.[21]

The goal of teaching the Bible in this understanding is to help individuals grow closer to God and be inspired (in-Spirited) to a transformed life of love and holy action. A key question in the educational process is this: *In what ways can I work to deepen and show my love and devotion in return for God's overwhelming love, known in the biblical texts and in Jesus Christ?*

The Bible gives a personal knowledge *of* God, rather than *about* God, a deep knowledge that leads "the knower into love, devotion and obedience."[22] The Bible confronts us with a Person, rather than being merely a collection of writings to be learned. These writings derive their unity from the theme of God's goodness and steadfast love, as opposed to human unfaithfulness. In goodness and love, God acts— saving, directing, even working through the devious. Through studying the Bible, we are enabled to be in the presence of God, to hear God's call and to respond in faith.[23] Thus the Bible is integral to the spiritual life of individuals and the community. Through descriptions of real relationships between God and people, the Bible offers spiritual insights for all.[24]

The central image in this approach is the God of goodness and faithfulness who loves us. This God judges but redeems; God no longer condemns but forgives. In the ancient spiritual traditions of Christianity, God who is holy yet forgiving calls us to an active life of holiness and forgiveness. The great mystics and saints of this tradition lived out their knowledge of God's goodness through a lifestyle of simplicity and charity, feeding the poor, tending the sick, and chastizing the church authorities when they were corrupt.[25]

The educational goal of growing closer to God can also be likened to the "imitation of Christ" (*imitatio Dei*) tradition within Christianity. Educationally, it leads to teaching believers how to pray the texts. It often includes instruction in classical methods of prayer and meditation, reflection on medieval mystics' understandings of biblical texts, and on the daily discipline of Bible readings (*lectio divina*), as reflected in the popular spirituality conferences and programs of our time. The many learners attending these conferences also benefit from an educational process of quiet reflection and journaling, along with group processes that include sharing their experiences of God's love in their lives.

The strength of this model is the emphasis on an intimate relationship with the loving God and on the imitation of Christ. Pastors have noticed in the midst of their congregations the often quiet, dedicated women and men who long for God with the passion of the psalmist and give many hours to the care of those who need help, through both secular and religious institutions. Educationally, this model provides a rich way of appropriating the biblical texts, through prayer and a daily discipline. It can also connect learners to the rich heritage we have in Christian mysticism. It is also effective because of the spiritual hunger present in contemporary society, as witnessed by the popularity of spirituality conferences and programs.[26]

Pastors complain, however, that many believers today seem to forget the action dimension of spirituality and psychologize biblical texts. They place the emphasis on God's goodness and forgiveness and forget the consequent call to act in light of our forgiveness and God's love. The result can be what is often called "feel-good spirituality." The call to act is seen as fulfilled in a change of attitude and personal feelings but is only weakly linked to new lifestyles and social transformation.

Those who truly follow this image of spiritual growth, though, do eventually find themselves engaged in God's ministry of reconciliation and love. Their key question, *In what ways can I work to deepen and show my love and devotion in return for God's overwhelming love*, pushes them from prayerful meditation on scripture out into the world to engage in thankful and loving action.

Conclusion

The Bible itself encourages the use of different images of God and a variety of educational models.[27] Different Christian traditions in different eras have emphasized one of these four models, but all are important to Christian faith. These approaches are indeed not necessarily exclusive, although they can be. Each model takes on central importance depending on the community, its tradition, its geographical setting, and its social-cultural context. It is understandable that poor, politically oppressed Latin American peasants and laborers find most meaning in the image of the God of justice and shalom. Likewise, in a society rich in material goods but poor in vision and meaning, such as the contemporary United States, the model of spiritual inspiration will find more fertile soil.

If each model, therefore, is valid, useful, and faithful to the gospel of Jesus Christ, we need not choose one above another. Rather, we may need first to name which one our community favors. Secondly, we may find it useful to notice differences held among adults in our church that correspond to differences among these models. By naming and describing these differences, adults can be helped to see some of the reasons for disagreement. They can learn to appreciate the validity of differing viewpoints. They may even come to understand that all four understandings enrich our knowledge of God and of ourselves. From one model, we learn of God's holiness and humanity's sinfulness, while from another we learn of God's presence in our community and our ability to experience God's Story in our lives. From one model, we hear the call to act for justice; from another we remember that we can act faithfully and tirelessly only when we are in close relationship to the loving God.

As we engage in Bible study, we will want to use all four models. As we discuss the meaning of biblical texts, we may need to name which set of understandings is guiding our thinking. In addition, if one set predominates, teachers can bring in the other models to stimulate thinking and learning. The identification and use of each of the models can broaden and deepen our study of the Bible and our knowledge of God. Ways in which we might do this will be found in chapter 3.

In sum, the goals of your Bible study will grow out of the central images of God and Bible held by your community at this time but will be shaped by the rich, multifaceted nature of the biblical materials as well. Furthermore, educational goals and methods become even more complex when we add the varied ways in which adults learn, as seen in the next chapter.

Four Models

Educational Goal	Biblical Image	Key Question
Conversion	Holy God and Sinful Humanity	In what ways do I need to repent and have my life transformed by the holy God?
Common Identity with Bible People	Community Stories Revealing God's Story	How do the biblical stories and our stories show God at work?
Justice and Faith in Action	God's Justice and Call for Social Transformation	What work do we need to do for justice and love of neighbor?
Spiritual Growth (Imitation of Christ)	God's Faithful Love	How can I deepen and show my love for God?

Chapter Two

Adults Learn Best When . . .

Buy truth, and do not sell it;
buy wisdom, instruction, and understanding.
Proverbs 23:23

> How can I get adults in my congregation to participate in adult education, especially Bible study? Why are so many of the adults in my class reluctant to enter into discussion? People ask for more Bible study in the church, and then, when we start new classes, few people come. Why is that?

"It has become evident that learners' reasons for participating in adult education are many, are complex, and are subject to change."[1]

Questions such as those above are being asked by both researchers and practitioners in the field of adult education. By understanding the adult learner, the artist/teacher should be able to develop and evaluate teaching strategies that will be effective. To understand adult learners is to understand what needs to go into the process of creating the canvas we call Bible study.

The quest to understand adults, how they learn

and grow and change, what their needs and desires are, has resulted in a large, complex body of literature. This chapter will attempt to summarize and clarify the research for the practitioner, without, it is hoped, oversimplifying a complex subject. Although theories of learning are not the same as theories of teaching, I will note some of their implications for teaching, which I will then develop in later chapters.

First, however, let us consider what we mean by the term "learning." To learn is to change, as in changing one's interpretation of an experience, or learning new or different behavior, or learning to feel differently about something. Learning takes on many forms.[2] Learning can be simple acquisition of new information, or it can involve reintegration of new understandings. It can teach us new skills, or it can convert our minds and hearts to an entirely new way of making sense of reality. It may be helpful to think of learning as a spiral, in which layers of new data and information enhance perception, deepen understanding, and ultimately can lead to major shifts in fundamental ways of understanding the world. Such a shift can be a total change in basic visions and understandings, in essence then, a new faith conversion.[3]

I have chosen to organize this material by answering the question, how do adults learn best? To answer this question, I have drawn on three sources: (1) documented research, (2) my experience as an adult educator in churches and theological institutions, and (3) data from the many pastors and church educators who participate in the Doctor of Ministry and Continuing Education programs that I have directed. From these sources the following picture (see chart on p. 49) develops of what enhances adult learning.[4]

The Learning Environment
Feels Safe and Supportive

Learning has an emotional nature to it.[5] Learning something new can frequently be painful or threatening. For a person to be able to deal with, rather than avoid, the discomfort that may come in the learning process, some environmental factors that lower the feeling of threat are needed.

In addition, learning and studying have often been associated with childhood.[6] Adults are reluctant to put themselves back into the dependent position of a child. They will avoid educational situations that reawaken feelings from childhood. They also often fear that they will fail if they do take the leap and engage in some educational endeavor.[7] Several factors can help create a supportive learning environment.

Respect for the Learner's Knowledge

Respect for the adult learner is stressed by Malcolm Knowles, Paulo Freire, and many other adult educators. Learners themselves will often voice preference for instructors "who respect me." This category includes, of course, courtesy and warmth. Freire speaks of the importance of teaching with love and humility.[8]

Respect includes another, perhaps more complex, attitude: true appreciation of the knowledge and experience that the learner already has. When we teach adults, we need to realize that each one brings a diversity of life experience and a wealth of knowledge to the class. Often adults are instructors themselves in other areas.[9]

Adults need affirmation for the knowledge they already have for two reasons. First, this affirmation provides psychological and emotional *support* and counters the fears of dependence that may surface. It keeps self-esteem high enough to motivate the learner to continue learning.[10] Second, and as important, this affirmation helps adults to *integrate* their previous knowledge with the new knowledge. They can thus explicitly as well as implicitly use information they have previously acquired.

Community

Community is crucial for *psychological* reasons. One role of the adult educator is "to help transform a collection of individuals into a cohesive group."[11] A community of people learning together provides emotional and intellectual support. The community provides a diversity of views, questions, and ideas. It offers each individual a mirror on him or herself. A learning community also reflects on itself and its own processes and learns from this reflection.[12]

Community is also crucial for *educational* reasons. Community shapes the values, attitudes, beliefs, and behavior of individuals. It teaches us "who we are" through its stories, rituals, assumptions, and attitudes. It passes on an entire worldview.[13] This learning on the part of the individuals in the community is often unconscious and unrecognized. It forms part of what is often called "tacit" learning or the "hidden curriculum."

Finally, and most importantly, community is crucial for teaching the Bible for *theological* reasons. "For where two or three are gathered in my name, I am there among them," said Jesus (Matt. 18:20). The Christian tradition affirms that in the community of faith the Holy Spirit is at work, and Jesus is revealed. Interpretation of the Bible and of faith stories and traditions, and decisions about moral and ethical principles and actions, are to take place in the community of faith. When individuals act alone, without the support and/or challenge of the community, individual pride and other sins can too easily lead one astray.[14]

In Christian community we should experience what is meant by such concepts as forgiveness, grace, love, and justice. Christian community is a place where we can experience a culture that is different from that of the contemporary world of individualism, secularism, and sectarianism. It is the place where we experience God's presence.[15]

Faithful Christian community is not necessarily a collection of people who think alike, look alike, or agree on all issues. Jesus provided the model: he gathered around himself a highly diverse community, women and men differing in occupation, education, and class. This group did not always agree, cooperate, or understand. But their loyalty to the Christ made of them a community. Likewise today, diversity and even disagreement can enrich and strengthen learning as we search together to follow Jesus Christ.

Collaboration

Adults in North American society have been raised in educational systems that encourage competition. Yet studies have long shown that when it comes to learning, students learn more when they work together. This reality is demonstrated in research laboratories, such as the scientific laboratories in Los Alamos, New Mexico. There, as in many other scientific institutions, physicists form research teams. Within these teams individuals work together cooperatively on scientific problems.

Collaboration in education can happen at two levels. The first is collaboration *among students*.[16] Educators have come to understand the wealth of learning that is available when learners share experience, insights, and vision with each other. Sometimes such learning is impeded when students themselves do not value what is learned from other students and count as valid only what is brought to the class by the teacher.

The second level of collaboration is *between teacher and student*. Many adult educators have come to see teaching as a collaborative effort with the students. Students are encouraged to set their own goals and to choose their own methods of learning. Knowles speaks of proactive, as opposed to reactive, learning, in which the teacher is a facilitator who helps release the students into inquiry and discovery.[17] Freire speaks of the teacher as a colearner and coinvestigator with the student.[18] In good education, the teacher is also learning.[19]

Many religious education classes lack collaboration on one or both of these levels. Sometimes collaboration is discouraged as the class searches for the "right" text or the "right" interpretation. Often a collaborative role for the teacher is inhibited, either by the teacher's desire to be authoritative or by the students' desire to have an expert, a "real" authority, provide them with answers. A collaborative approach in studying the Bible, on the other hand, allows for diversity of questions and ideas and deepens the possibility of creative, revelatory insight.

Mentor or Model

Learning can be strengthened when a person has a mentor who works closely with him or her.[20] A mentor is not simply an older person who is a model for the learner. All through life, other individuals help adults learn: they function as *guides* who show the path and warn of dangers, as *models* demonstrating appropriate and helpful behavior and ways of thinking, as *advocates* who work on their behalf, as *coaches* who challenge and demand.[21]

The Christian tradition is rich with images of the mentor and/or model: the older pilgrim who helps the younger over the rough road; the spiritual guide who counsels the person of faith; the confessor who helps the process of self-examination, repentance, restitution, and forgiveness; the parent who even beyond childhood models responsibility and wisdom; the Christ who is not only our Savior but our brother and friend on the way.

Pastors and adult educators function in all these ways for adults. One pastor discovered in studying his congregation that his most eager adult learners attended classes or church events because of their trust and confidence in their pastor. They did not wish to choose or shape these learning events: they saw their pastor as mentor and guide in this process.[22]

The core of good teaching with adult learners is care, as this study and other research demonstrate. Adult education deals with the whole person and grows out of relationships, even more than content.[23]

Good Organization and Attractive Environment

Many researchers emphasize the importance of the organizational structure for learning.[24] If the atmosphere is warm and friendly, learners feel more welcome. If the facilities are comfortable and attractive, learning seems more interesting and exciting. Knowles tells the story of a class that met in a dingy and dull basement room. By the third meeting, it was clear to him that the class was not going well. After some discussion, the group decided to brighten up the environment with paper mobiles and other hand-made, inexpensive decorations. The change in mood, energy, and hence in learning was remarkable.[25]

This story is an object lesson for church groups. While church educators work hard to brighten the classrooms used by children, adults often find them-selves in basement rooms, out-of-the-way corners, or large, empty fellowship halls with scratched black-boards, old furniture, and echoing floors. It can be hard to hear, to see the blackboard, or to engage in discussion. All of these factors are important ones in the ability of adults to engage in learning.

Schedules also need to be clear and consistent. One of the major reasons adults do not participate in educational activities has proven to be lack of clear information about those activities.[26] Advance prepa-ration and care for details are important bases of good organization. In my experience as an adminis-trator of adult education programs, I have found that comfort, structure, and clear information matter a great deal to the adult. When these are attended to, the learner is appreciative and is better able to learn.

In order for the environment to be supportive, the educational organization must truly value human beings and their development.[27] This value must be at the heart of religious education for adults. This is not always the case, however. We need to reflect God's love for God's children by giving as much value to our people as to our subject (the Bible) or our institution (the church).

To call for a supportive learning environment is not to call for learning that is devoid of challenge, interest, diversity, and even tension. On the contrary, a pleasing learning environment helps set the stage for getting adults interested and connected with the subject matter.

Their Interest Is Engaged

The myth lingers in our society that once one is an adult, one stops learning. "You can't teach an old dog new tricks" is sometimes applied to anyone over the age of thirty.[28]

Studies in adult intelligence tell a different story. Researchers describe two kinds of adult intelligence: fluid intelligence and crystallized intelligence.[29] Fluid intelligence can be characterized as the ability to process information, form concepts, and think abstractly. Fluid intelligence is often seen in short-term memory, word analogies, and verbal reasoning. It is what is sometimes seen as "quick intelligence," the "off-the-top-of-the-head" knowledge. It seems to have a neurophysical base in heredity and health. Studies show that this type of intelligence is highest in young adulthood, but basically stays the same throughout adulthood. It can decline with bad health or loss of hearing or eyesight.

Crystallized intelligence, on the other hand, increases with age. It is based on what adults learn through experience, formal schooling, work, and acculturation. It is the mix of fluid intelligence with cultural and personal knowledge. Crystallized intelligence gives the adult the ability to test well in areas of information storage, verbal comprehension, and numerical reasoning.[30]

The results of research in this area show that adult learning does not necessarily decline with age. Indeed it can increase when the need to learn is great. However, older adults rely more on crystallized intelligence than fluid intelligence. They "substitute wisdom for brilliance."[31] Older adults can learn as well as younger adults on condition that they can regulate the pace to be neither too fast nor too slow, and that their interest, based in crystallized intelligence, gets engaged.

Several catalysts serve to engage the mind of the adult: cognitive dissonance, layers of reflection, and openness to the unexpected.

The Challenge of Cognitive Dissonance

Cognitive dissonance can be defined as the clash of what a person knows or believes with new, conflicting knowledge or beliefs. Many adult educators agree that sometimes dissonance is necessary to learning.[32] It presents adults with a challenge, which can help to make education more meaningful and to push adults onward to more learning.[33] Perhaps this is because people enjoy a puzzle and do not like to leave it unsolved. Cognitive dissonance, thus, "may stimulate new discoveries and may inaugurate a realignment of the whole system in a more realistic and coherent way."[34]

At the same time, too great a challenge or experience of cognitive dissonance can prove counterproductive and even harmful. In this situation adults often either withdraw from the educational activity or deny that conflict exists.[35] Some religious groups even work to help their members avoid learning by lowering cognitive dissonance among their believers and helping them avoid dealing with reality or resolving conflict. Such religious education is not true education but simply a reinforcer of ideology and unexamined beliefs. Critical reflection, therefore, that allows us to examine our personal beliefs is essential for good education.[36]

Layers of Reflection[37]

Reflection is repeated analysis of our understanding, experience, and feelings about something we are studying. Reflection that is repeated and shared in discussion, with increasing depth of analysis and evaluation, greatly benefits adult learners. One example in the parish illustrates how this can work.

Example

Participants in a group studying the Episcopal *Book of Common Prayer* were being trained by their pastor to engage in theological reflection.[38] He devised for the group a certain series of reflective questions with which to examine the worship service of the Lord's Supper. The same questions were used every week to examine different parts of the service. Each participant thought individually about the questions at home. Then the group would together go over the same questions. The reflective nature of the questions, the act of reflecting first alone and then a second time with the group, and the refusal of the pastor to provide "the right answers" pushed them to more critical analysis. This process led to interesting discoveries by the participants of the group. They found themselves hearing new meanings in the prayers, which led them to reexamine and rework their own religious beliefs. These adults, filled with excitement by what they had each learned, were galvanized into action and became an important force for creative ministry in the church.[39]

The *content* of reflection is repetitive thinking about the subject matter, often in question form. The first act of reflection is often simply remembering the knowledge being learned. The second reflection introduces analysis of the material in light of the learner's experience, and assessment of what has been learned and how the learner is thereby changed. The third reflection can push to a critical consciousness of how the learner's world is reshaped by this learning.

The *process* of reflection is strengthened by repetition, articulation (that is, saying what one is thinking either out loud or on paper), and group discussion.[40] The repetitive rhythm, the time to think and feel, and the act of sharing all contribute to helping knowledge grow and crystallize.

Openness to the Unexpected

Many educators point out that often the most valuable learning is that which is unexpected. It is often labeled the "latent" content or the "hidden" curriculum. In both cases, this is the learning that is "caught" rather than "taught." It involves attitudes, values, and emotions as well as intellectual material. It is often unplanned and may affect the learner on an unconscious level.

At the same time, the unexpected can also mean the conscious surprises, the "aha!" moments, the detours in the conversation that help everything make sense. This unexpected learning can happen as a gestalt, a sudden vision of the whole.

The unexpected can help in the creation of "memorable encounters" that some consider so important in adult education.[41] Yet certain kinds of teaching—such as an overly rigid adherence to behavioral goals and extremely structured lesson plans—can keep the unexpected from happening. Adult attitudes, if they are rigid and inflexible, can also inhibit these wonderful moments that are the Spirit's gifts.

The teacher's art, in sum, is to hold together flexibility and structure in such a way to allow unexpected insights to occur. This art grows from the teacher's own openness to the guidance of the Spirit and from her knowledge of her adult students. This knowledge needs to include awareness of the life experience of these students, as we see next.

Their Learning Is Grounded in Their Experience

The work of Malcolm Knowles and his associates has stressed that a major difference between children and adults is the wealth of knowledge based in experience that adults have. Adults shape their self-identity and define themselves by their experience: "I studied at . . . , worked at . . . , lived in . . . , moved to . . ." We have also seen above that adults increase their use of crystallized intelligence in order to learn. This intelligence grows out of years of education and experience.

Adult experience also can become a barrier to learning by creating biases and knowledge that need to be unlearned.[42] Researchers have studied the problem of interference in learning from previous inaccurate learning.[43]

Good adult education must therefore take this adult experience into account. Researchers note that adults prefer (1) learning that applies to life situations here and now, (2) being listened to as knowers, and (3) having their needs met.

Learning That Applies to Life Situations Here and Now

As adults mature they "organize their learning around life problems."[44] These problems may be developmental ones that grow out of aging, work advancement, marriage, and family. They may grow out of the society or personal crises. Likewise they engage in new learning more effectively when it is set in the context of real-life situations. Literacy programs are good examples. When adults are taught to read using arbitrary vocabulary lists, the results are disappointing. When the vocabulary is that of everyday work and life situations, the results improve dramatically.

This understanding may imply that there are some times in individual adult lives when they are more motivated than other times to engage in religious education or study the Bible. One task of religious educators is to identify the life situations toward which Bible study can speak. Another possibility is to make sure that study of the Bible relates to immediate life situations of the participants.

Being Treated as Knowers

We have seen above that one element of a safe learning climate is for the adult to be treated with respect. This respect includes the recognition of the wealth of knowledge that each adult has accumulated. What does this mean for teaching in the church?

First, the experience of adults means that a class will be very heterogeneous. Adults in one class will have a range of learning styles, motivations, and attitudes. For the teacher, this variety poses a challenge and encourages a range of teaching styles. For the adult learner, this variety is also a potential problem. The challenge is having to deal with many different points of view and different needs. At the same time, if adults are seen as "knowers," these differences can provide more insight, more interesting questions, and more creative problem solving.

Second, teachers need to recognize that contemporary adults are often well educated and critical and that they have access to a lot of information.[45] At the same time, they may know very little about the Bible (although they may think they know more than they do!). Therefore adults resent teaching that treats them as children who do not know anything. They tend to prefer experiential pedagogy such as discussion, challenging lectures, and problem-solving activities, in which they can use their experience with the new learning.[46]

Third, adult knowledge needs to be understood as being more than knowledge gained in formal education. As stated earlier, it is clear that adults continue to learn throughout their lives and that this learning takes a variety of forms, both formal and informal. In the church, this means teaching the Bible in all sorts of settings: not only in formal classes but also in prayers, at meals, on mission trips, in worship, and so on.

Having Their Needs Met

Adult education literature is filled with discussion, and some disagreement, about the pressure to meet adult needs. Studies show that adults seek to learn most when they have immediate problems to solve, such as how to get a promotion, how to take care of a newborn baby, or how to deal with cancer. These needs can come from outside pressures such as work. However, some educators see inner pressures, such as self-esteem and quality of life, as the greater motivators.[47]

This last interpretation of "needs" opens the door more widely for religious education and the Bible. Educators acknowledge that the most important adult task is to create meaning out of life experiences.[48] In addition, adult development into more complex ways of thinking may push adults to rework previously acquired knowledge that is important to their lives. Needs, therefore, can include the search for a deepening of complex thinking, of self-esteem, and of meaning making.

An important critique of needs-based learning is that it is overly consumerist and stresses "giving learners what they say they want."[49] Educational effectiveness is then judged by how happy it makes the learners. Yet popularity and contentment may not be good measures of true education. Good teachers often help learners break out of the familiar ways of thinking. In addition, learners may not be the best judges of their own needs. A deeper need may involve wrestling with personal meaning and self-concept in a critical, uncomfortable manner.

The church needs especially to take this caution to heart as it struggles to make adult education more popular. We must live with the tension of helping adults meet immediate needs while at the same time urging them on to more critical reflection and/or to deeper meaning making. Both these levels of understanding of adult needs are important for teaching the Bible. Sometimes we neglect immediate concrete needs of adults in our churches in the quest to help them work on their deepest needs, those of faith and belief. Often the door to this second level lies in the first level of immediate needs. At the same time, the church is rightly aware that immediate needs may hide more profound ones, matters of meaning and faith.

One of the most important experiences of adulthood is learning and liking to be in control of one's life as much as possible. This adult need to direct one's own life and not be directed by others is an important factor in teaching and learning and will be addressed next.

They Are Self-directed

Studies suggest that most adult learning happens for self-directed adults. A need arises, and adults set about to learn in order to meet that need, for example, the young woman who wants to learn how to change the oil in her car herself so that she can save money. When this adult sets out to learn, she will choose from a variety of resources, human and non-human. She may read a book, ask a friend for a demonstration, rent a videotape, or enroll in a class. Learning, in this case, is directed by the adult in many ways. She chooses the method of learning she prefers, the instructor, and the goal. Even when she signs up for a formal class, our adult learner pursues her own goals. Many adult educators conclude that adults learn best when they are allowed to be, even encouraged to be, self-directed. Self-direction has several important dimensions: (1) learning how to learn, (2) having some control over the learning process, and (3) unlearning inaccurate knowledge and dysfunctional habits.

Learning How to Learn

Educators of adults agree that a major task of good adult education is to help adults become aware of how they each learn best. Adults can be helped to develop learning skills in these areas: use of resources, identification of effective strategies of learning, self-evaluation, and personal attitude.[50]

Adults can be helped to identify what the *resources* are in a certain field. They can learn both how to choose those resources that are most useful for them and how to use them "proactively."[51] Adults without computer knowledge, for example, tend to prefer using Bible atlases, dictionaries, or videos available in the library. Some adults may desire instruction in new technologies and resources.

Generations born after 1967, however, tend to prefer using electronic tools to learn. These computer-literate adults may avoid study of the Bible until they discover the many computer-based tools for studying the Bible that have been developed. We can now put the entire Bible and Bible concordances on a CD-ROM, and call them up on our computers. Bible games, Greek language programs, and Internet Web sites also exist. These individuals will also need the church to help them evaluate the accuracy and helpfulness of the myriad Web sites that are being created.

Educators can also identify human resources such as the retired pastor, the local rabbi, and the congregational member who has slides from his trip to biblical lands. Important human resources also include the personal knowledge and experience of other adult peers. These resources need special emphasis by the educator.[52]

Educators can also help adults identify their *learning preferences*. The effective learner is the one who has reflected on his or her preferred methods of learning. For one person it is lecture combined with discussion, for another it is reading. A third learns best with visual aids such as outlines or videotapes. Another prefers informal discussion with people who are experts in that area. Good learners have learned which strategies are more effective for them. They also know to change strategies with different areas of study if necessary. A person would not learn to cook exotic dishes using the same learning strategies as learning to read biblical Hebrew, for example. The effective learner knows her best ways to learn and in both cases might choose strategies that involve, for example, discussion and repetition, strategies that work well for her.

Another important way to get at differences in how people learn is to attend to the "multiple-intelligences" theory. This theory grows out of research showing that individuals process information and think in many different ways. The seven intelligences described are linguistic, logical-mathematical, spatial, musical, bodily-kinesthetic, interpersonal, and intrapersonal. Other kinds may exist, and these may be grouped together differently by different intellects. The central point for these researchers is "to make the case for the plurality of intellect."[53] People will use many of these together and change what they use most over a lifetime. Good teachers of adults take these different intelligences into account in planning their teaching.

To learn how to learn involves also frequent *self-evaluation*. Reflection upon progress towards one's goal or upon the educational process helps the adult learner to be more self-directed and in control of the learning process. Such evaluation can be added to any curriculum and engaged in by individuals or groups.[54]

Finally, *attitude* is important for adult learning. "Adults must believe that they can learn, or they won't,"[55] states one researcher. Studies show that adults who had bad educational experiences previously have a more difficult time with formal educational processes. Adults who believe that they cannot learn do not. I have found evidence that anxiety about learning about the Bible may keep adults from joining Bible study classes.

Having Control Over the Learning Process

One way to help adults overcome their anxiety about education is to help them feel that they have some control over their learning. This control can be facilitated in several areas: subject and content of study, organization, learning methods, and learning goals. For Knowles and his followers, this point is critical and has the following implications for religious education: adult learners should be part of the planning of the religious education program; adult learners can help administer the program; adult learners can help evaluate the program; adult learners need to have choices; and adult learners are important resources.[56]

Unlearning Inaccurate Knowledge and Dysfunctional Habits

Old learning can interfere with new learning.[57] Adults who experience interference must unlearn previously learned material before they can learn the new material. This makes learning slower and more difficult. Yet, with the rapid increase in knowledge, this kind of unlearning and relearning is not uncommon. For example, some of the scientific "facts" that many of us learned in school as children are no longer believed to be true. With every science article we read, we find ourselves not only learning but also having to unlearn our previous knowledge.

In addition to previous knowledge, previous learning strategies may prove no longer to be beneficial. These strategies may actually interfere with our learning and need to be unlearned. New strategies must then be developed. For example, an adult may have always appropriated religious material in an unquestioning, fully accepting manner, by listening to or reading articles written by religious authorities. As a more mature adult, confronted with differing opinions from different religious authorities, the adult will need to learn a new strategy. The old, unquestioning acceptance of whatever is presented will no longer work. A new manner of learning, through dialogue and questions, will be more effective.

I believe that "unlearning" is a critical part of studying the Bible. Much of what adults know about the Bible, and how they know it, they learned as children. These learnings are filled with childhood misconceptions, preformal reasoning, and simplistic understandings. The way in which they have learned biblical texts are not always useful to them later on. In addition, the biblical knowledge of adults is shaped by cultural references that have often stereotyped and distorted the true biblical story. We will return to this point, the importance of unlearning, in later chapters.

Education Speaks to Mind, Heart, and Soul

Up to this point, our discussion has drawn from studies of adult learning in which analysis, reasoning, and critique were emphasized. But in these studies hints of other ways of learning and knowing have appeared. Knowing that is creative, intuitive, contemplative, and imaginative is being explored in secular education, based in part on earlier work on human creativity and imagination by thinkers such as Jerome Bruner, Arthur Koestler, Amos Wilder, and Paul Ricoeur. In religious education, scholars such as Maria Harris, Nelle Morton, and Thomas Groome have explored the importance of imagination, story, and symbol for religious learning.

The role of symbol, story, and imagination is so important in adult learning and study of the Bible that we will explore it more fully in chapter 4. To complete the picture of how adults learn best, we note the following observations: (1) adults need to encounter symbol and story; (2) adults need to be encouraged to use their imagination; (3) adults need to live their knowledge in ritual and action.

The Need of Adults
to Encounter Symbol and Story

Walter Brueggemann hypothesizes that the role of story in the Bible is to answer the question of identity. The answer to the query, "What do these stones mean?" (Josh. 4:21) is the story of God's liberation of a group of slaves in Egypt and of making them the people of the covenant.[58] For Christians, the answer to the question of the crowd on Pentecost, "What does this mean?" (Acts 2:12) is the story of Jesus Christ as told there by Peter (Acts 2:22–24). Behind the kerygmatic formula at the heart of Christian identity, "Jesus Christ is my Lord and Savior," lies the story of God's work through Jesus Christ and how that affects our lives.

Symbols are another important aspect of our understanding. They are found in stories, but also apart from story. They carry many layers of meaning that can never be completely explained. The cross, bread, water, and wine are all central symbols in the Christian faith. What keeps these symbols alive and meaningful are the stories (and the rituals, as we see below) they spring from: the resurrection of Christ, the feeding of the multitudes and the Last Supper, John's baptism and Jesus' washing of feet, and so on.

People's lives are filled with stories and symbols. People often think of their lives in narrative and story form: "I was born in . . . , the child of . . . , I am the product of . . ." Families form identities around happenings that they shape into stories. "Do you remember when the dog ate all the Christmas decorations and . . . ?" Families also develop symbols that are important to them, such as a certain kind of angel for the top of the Christmas tree or a nickname that symbolizes the family.

The Bible is filled with symbol and story. Adults as much as children enjoy and remember stories and symbols. As many religious educators have noted, one goal of teaching the Bible is to help them bring their personal stories together with the biblical stories.

The Need of Adults to Be Encouraged to Use Their Imagination

Researchers find that imagination is a critical ingredient of creative thinking. In science, for example, imagination in the form of dreams and images led to such discoveries as the circular benzene molecule and the DNA double helix.[59] Imagination triggered by metaphors and symbols not only allows for new inventions, it opens the door to new questions and insights. In literature also, images, symbols, and metaphors lie at the heart of poetry and prose. The Bible is rich with these elements that are meant to spark vision and imagination.

Disciplined imagination, called midrash, was used for centuries by Jewish rabbis to open up and interpret biblical texts. While some of these interpretations seem far-fetched and archaic to us today, the principle of imaginative interpretation remains central. When participants in Bible study are invited to enter into biblical story and images and "play" with them imaginatively, they discover both excitement and meaning in the text. Imaginative interpretation, coupled with critical reflection, allows for a disciplined imagination that can be insightful in the contemporary context and faithful to the biblical text.

The Need of Adults to Live Their Knowledge in Ritual and Action

Educators have observed that action is necessary for true learning. Many educators stress the need to combine action and reflection. The goal of reflection, especially critical reflection, is new action that leads to new reflection and renewed action, in a repetitive cycle.

Action can initiate learning and lead to deeper understanding. This happens, for example,[60] in churches when a mission project, such as repairing a house in a poor neighborhood, leads participants to see the biblical texts and prayers shared by the pastor in a new light.

Another important form of action in religious matters is ritual. Judith Plaskow, a Jewish theologian, states that ritual is what changes story into sacred text. Ritual allows the past to become living memory in the present.[61] In praying the Psalms, hearing the scriptures read in worship, using biblical texts for worship in class, meditating on a passage, the literary texts become scripture.

A third important form of action is behavior in everyday living, particularly moral behavior. What are we called to do out as a result of these texts? If such a call is not evident (some texts do not directly result in action), how can I evaluate my actions, attitudes, beliefs, and values in light of this text? How does it help me reflect on the beliefs and behavior of my society? Such questions push the learner to combine reflection with action and to integrate more deeply knowledge and experience.

Conclusion

Many factors affect adult learning. We pastors and religious educators must be more attentive to how adults learn. We need to consider seriously the learning environment and the most profitable use for our learners of a wide variety of resources. Most critical to helping adults learn are these factors: the focus on adult needs, immediate and long-term; the encouragement of more self-direction in learning; the promotion of layers of reflection on the material; and the movement toward critical and imaginative thinking.

Now that we have looked at goals drawn from our understanding of the Word of God and at the nature of adult learning, we must turn to what this all means for teaching. The artist/teacher now better understands the two texts, Bible and adults, that he is hoping to connect. The art will come in painting, a process that brings meaning to the learners and inspires them to greater faithfulness as Christ's disciples. In the next chapter, I will describe a teaching model that has proved to be helpful for the art of teaching the Bible.

Adults Learn Best When . . .

A. The learning environment feels safe and supportive through
   1. respect
   2. community
   3. collaboration
   4. mentors or models
   5. good organization
B. Their interest is engaged through
   1. the challenge of cognitive dissonance
   2. layers of reflection
   3. openness to the unexpected
C. Their learning is grounded in their experience by
   1. application to life situations here and now
   2. being treated as knowers
   3. having their needs met
D. They are self-directed by
   1. learning how to learn
   2. having control over the learning process
   3. unlearning inaccurate knowledge and dysfunctional habits
   4. engaging in self-evaluation
E. Their education speaks to mind, heart, and soul through
   1. symbol and story
   2. imagination
   3. ritual and action

Chapter Three

The Five Rs Model
of Bible Study

Now that we have explored some issues concerning the Bible in chapter 1 and about adult learning in chapter 2, we teachers are faced with the challenge of creating an effective teaching process. Through this teaching process, we hope that the two "texts" will connect: the text of the Bible and the text of the lives of the adult students.

In this chapter, I describe a model for teaching the Bible that I have developed and used. It consists of five steps, the five Rs, that provide teaching methods and activities. These five R steps are a guide for the artist/teacher, providing suggestions for colors and techniques, but are designed to be flexible and spread over time. The artist/teacher's art, that is, the teaching process, will also be shaped by the particularities of the study group and the biblical texts.

The ultimate goal of the five Rs model is based in the Christian belief that the Bible is God's Word for us humans and essential for the Christian life. The five Rs therefore aim to engage learners with their minds, emotions, and wills, so that heart and life can be open to God, wherever they are in their Christian pilgrimage. Each step of the model will be discussed educationally and theologically and will be described, with concrete examples to guide the educator.

This model begins with prayer. The Holy Spirit, the source of inspiration for our sacred scriptures, is invited to inspire us today. Prayers and songs of praise, thanksgivings for God's gift of these scriptures, quiet moments to remember that we live in God's presence—all can begin this study.

Remembering

As the adults enter the room, they notice old Sunday school pictures and reproductions of art classics that depict the biblical passages about to be studied. Music is playing, familiar to some, in which allusions or direct references are made to the text. Novels and poetry that can be connected to the biblical texts decorate a side table. Before the participants open the Bible, the teacher begins with prayer and invites participants to think about what they remember—from their childhood or from art and music—about the biblical story or passage about to be studied. A list is compiled either on the board or newsprint.

The arts and literature of Western civilization have, until recently, been dominated by the Christian church and therefore are laden with biblical references and imagery. Contemporary American culture, even in this "post-Christian," "post-modern" period, still contains many references to the Bible.[1] These references carry with them certain images and understandings of the meaning of that story or passage. Adults raised in this culture may have their understandings of the Bible texts shaped by these cultural images. Some adults carry ideas from literature: Milton's *Paradise Lost*, Steinbeck's *East of Eden*, Wilder's

The Skin of Our Teeth, for example; others remember images from art in church and museums; others cannot quite shake out of their mind the movie images, such as Charlton Heston in *The Ten Commandments*.

Adult learners raised in the church also have memories of the meaning of texts based in their childhood. They remember the simplified stories from Sunday school of Noah's ark, Abraham and Sarah (often without Hagar), Joseph and his coat, Moses and the Red Sea, songs like the Byrds' "To Everything There Is a Season" from Ecclesiastes. These old understandings can date from a preabstract period of cognitive formation and may not have matured as the individual matured. In addition, these conceptions of the passage were developed in a different social-cultural era, and often in a very different church environment.

In this first step, adults are invited to think about what they already know. With some passages, not much will be remembered; with others, especially for stories and some psalms, many recollections will emerge. Adults are often surprised at how much they know about a text. Some will even remember actual verses (older adults often remember lines from the King James Version that was used in their childhood). Two levels of remembering are involved: remembering what the individual knows and remembering references and stereotypes that float around this culture. The list that is generated will reflect both.

The step of remembering helps adult learners in several of the areas described in chapter 2. First, it allows them to be treated as knowers, as contributors that have some knowledge and experience that they are bringing to the discussion. Second, sharing builds community. Variety and diversity in the community are acknowledged from the beginning as a positive factor that will enrich the Bible study. Different understandings of the Bible (see chapter 1) may begin to emerge at this point. Third, the learner's interest is immediately engaged and a first layer of reflection on the text is introduced. Remembering initiates reflection that involves both mind and emotion as people share their past experience with this passage. For some this biblical text may have left faint memories of a saying, a character, a verse—if anything at all is remembered. For others, this passage—or a verse or a biblical person—may have had important meaning at one time and may still carry importance. Some adults may hold deep feelings of ambivalence or even dislike of a passage due to a bad childhood experience. Remembering allows persons to get at these memories and to reconnect with them, thereby making a deeper reflection possible.

Another important educational reason for this step is that it can facilitate "unlearning" if it is necessary (see chapter 2). By setting out what they know, adults are able to analyze, evaluate, and rethink their "old" knowledge as they proceed through the Bible study. As they move more deeply into the study, they may notice that some of their previous understandings were literal and concrete in a way that is characteristic of elementary school children who are not yet able to think abstractly. The adult ability to think abstractly and with metaphors and symbols will be engaged in the course of the study and will clash with the more concrete understandings of childhood.

The step of remembering begins a process that allows these preabstract understandings to be named and set out for later evaluation. This comparison of old and new knowledge creates a conflict (the cognitive dissonance described in chapter 2) that helps the process of unlearning. It also helps deal with adult resistance to new interpretations and the feelings of threat that are caused by this conflict.

This step is helpful for theological reasons as well.[2] As we have seen in chapter 1, people bring different perspectives about the Bible and even different goals to Bible study. Everyone, however, aims to listen deeply to the text and be nurtured or changed by this experience. Each desires to hear God's word to them. When adults come to a biblical text with old understandings, they can fail to hear God's word to them for this time in a new way. Their human experience creates a veil that can hide God's word. This step of remembering allows this veil to be identified and lifted aside so that the biblical text is heard more clearly, in deeper, new ways, guided by the Holy Spirit.[3]

Examples

A. *Study of John:* A refreshing way to study the Gospel of John is to focus on the actions of the disciples as models of different kinds of faithfulness. The traditional method of studying Jesus' discourses in John is set aside and the focus is on how the faithfulness of the disciples helps Jesus' ministry of bringing light into the world (John 1). A study of the stories of the followers of Jesus, from Mary his mother to Mary Magdalene, leads the readers into almost every chapter in John and can result in deeper understanding of the discourses.[4] The step of remembering is especially helpful when it comes to characters in the biblical stories.

For example, to begin a study of John 11, the story of Martha, Mary, and Lazarus (and, in passing, of

Thomas and the other disciples), make a list of all the characteristics of these disciples, especially some of the stereotypes (those for Thomas, Martha, and Mary are best known). Who are the characters in this story? Where are they from? What does the class remember of this story? What art do people remember that illustrates this story? What verses come to mind? (In every group I have taught, someone remembers, "He stinketh.") What sermons have they heard about these people or this situation? What feelings do they have about this text? Make a list on newsprint or a board for later evaluation.

B. *Study of the pastoral epistles (1 and 2 Timothy, Titus):* The class may remember little that is good from these epistles (letters). Women often remember the uncomfortable injunction to "learn in silence with full submission" (1 Tim. 2:11). Others may remember verses about slaves or the mention of elders, deacons, and bishops. A few might remember the often quoted "all scripture is inspired by God and is useful for teaching" (2 Tim. 3:16). An interesting, but perhaps short, list, is compiled.

Revisiting the Text

Now it is time to listen carefully to the text. Adult participants are asked to read the study passage carefully to themselves. One, or several, readers read it out loud. A few minutes of silence are built in for the learners to think, jot notes, underline words or verses of interest, or to journal. During this quiet time of reflection, the teacher hands out or lists questions to be explored. Concordances and commentaries are placed in the room. Especially useful and colorful are resources pulled from the youth room, such as atlases and Bible dictionaries. Encyclopedias that illustrate the plants, animals, food, clothes, and other artifacts mentioned in the Bible are also interesting for adults. Adults visit the text again and again as they explore the story behind and the content in the text. Individuals or groups share their discoveries and engage in discussion together, answering each others' questions, listing more questions to research.

This second step guides the learners to be extremely attentive to the actual, written text and will often be carried out over several class sessions. The goal is to revisit the text a number of times, going deeper each time, and in the process learning some simple tools of Bible study used by scholars and pastors. Teaching adults how to use these tools empowers adults by opening to them a mature study of the Bible. It demonstrates that they are respected as learners who are capable of learning these methods of study and of understanding the complex questions raised when they are used.

This step is an initial move toward interpretation. The step of revisiting the text using professional tools begins addressing two of the basic principles of biblical interpretation: *(1) Biblical texts must be understood within their historical and cultural context; (2) Biblical texts must be read within the framework of the larger text.*[5] These principles of interpretation allow the achievement of each of our goals for Bible study as described in chapter 1.

Revisiting the text begins in a variety of ways. For example, someone reads while the rest listen; then all read the text silently to themselves. The teacher then hands out some historical and literary questions often used by scholars and invites groups or individuals to search for answers in the resources provided. Bible dictionaries, concordances, study Bibles, different

Bible translations, some easy commentaries, Sunday school study guides—all these are laid out for use in the classroom. The teacher also solicits questions from the adults.

The historical and contextual questions are usually asked in two ways: behind-the-text questions and in-the-text questions.[6] The *behind-the-text* questions are historical. The simple *w* questions—who, what, when, where, and why—can serve as guides. Who wrote the text? Who was the audience? When and where was it written (it may have been written long after the period of time it reflects and in a different land)? Does it reflect the period it writes about accurately? What does it emphasize or leave out from that period? Why was the author writing it?

In-the-text questions are about the literary shape of the text: the story and/or words in it. These questions assume that how the text is written matters a great deal for the meaning. Every word and phrase, each sequence of events, the description of characters and settings, the movement to a literary climax in a story—all of these are purposefully structured to give meaning and feeling to the passage. In-the-text questions explore the *how* questions: How does this narrative, or how do these verses, work? How does this passage relate to the whole chapter, the whole book, and the whole Bible? Four main elements can be identified and investigated: key words, actions, dialogue, and narration. Exploring these elements helps address the *how* questions and allows adults to begin to explore the meaning of the text.[7] Useful to this discussion can be different translations of the passage.

These general questions can and should be shaped by the particular interests and concerns of the adults who are investigating this text. They may have many questions: What does this word mean? Where was this tribe of Israel living and why was it at war? Who are these people called Pharisees? What is a psalm? In an environment filled with useful resources, from atlases to computer concordances, and in an investigative questioning atmosphere, adults will eventually gather the courage to ask these questions and to start searching for the answers.

The teacher's role is to stimulate these questions and provide resources for research. The teacher is not a passive, nonspeaking voice. Whether a pastor or a lay leader, the teacher clearly has made significant preparations in order to help develop skills: skills in asking questions, skills in looking for answers. A lecture can be as valid a way to bring information as a concordance search, a video, or a discussion. The key is the attitude of the teacher: an attitude of deep listening to the learners in order to draw out of them their questions.

These historical and literary questions necessitate revisiting the text several times. Levels of reflection that grow progressively deeper and more complex are thereby built into the educational process. Historical-contextual data are gathered, and the passage is set in a larger context. Questions such as "Why do we feel that we need to know this information to understand this text?" "Does it matter whether Paul wrote this text or not?" "Why do we need to understand the Pharisees better?" "Does it make a difference when the psalms were written and for whom?" "What was the relationship between Jews and Samaritans and between men and women, especially in public?" "What were the food laws and who kept them?"—all are important to deeper delving.

The second principle of biblical interpretation—reading the smaller text within the context of the larger passage—can also be explored. Cross-references to other biblical texts are checked: Where else is this phrase found? What part of the Old Testament is being quoted or alluded to? How is what is quoted here different from the original text? Research assignments need to be very specific and focused (each small group might be given one key word to research, or a different related text to explore, or a different commentary to check).

Exploring and developing questions about the text, both behind and within, teach adults some of the basic skills that scholars and pastors have believed for more than a century are essential for those who want to listen to the word of God.

Examples

A. *Study of John:* Ask participants to listen carefully to this long passage, John 11:1–47, as it is being read. Build in silence, for reflection and journaling. Then begin class exploration and discussion. List questions and assign them to individuals or small groups, depending on the size of the class. Distribute the most helpful resources to research the assigned question (for example, if the question is "Where is Bethany and where did Jesus travel to?" an atlas is given to that group or individual). The first set of questions are the *behind*-the-text questions; these may have been addressed earlier and, if so, can be skipped (who wrote the Gospel, when, why, and so on). Then address questions *in* the text: Who are the main characters? Who does the most talking? Whom does Jesus talk with the most? What patterns in action do you find? What was the Jewish attitude toward death at the time of Jesus? Questions of literary structure are introduced. The teacher or a learner may note, for example, the preeminence of Martha in this story ("Jesus loved Martha and her sister . . ." [v. 5]); the threefold affirmation of faith, given first by Martha, then by Mary; the parallels between Martha in this passage and Peter in the Synoptic Gospels, and the differences; the similarities and differences between Jesus and Elijah). Encourage discussion of what everyone is discovering in this passage, even when these discoveries may disagree with each other.

B. *Study of the Pastoral Epistles:* The historical-contextual questions are especially critical for these letters, due to the controversial nature of some of the passages. Most scholars do not believe these were written by Paul (which is a source of discomfort to many of our members and merits discussion). However, they are scripture, whether or not Paul was the author. Therefore, it is important, as the controversial passages on women, slaves, and church leadership are encountered, that the historical questions (what, when, and for whom were these written) and the larger text questions (what is the overall purpose of the letters) be explored. Knowing that the author is attempting to convince the church to stop squabbling and to demonstrate Christ's love to the world by acting it out and by being culturally appropriate (hence passages about slaves and women) guides learners as they move into deeper interpretation.

Reflecting Critically

In this step, the study group thinks carefully about two texts and how they meet: the texts of their lives and the Bible texts. The teacher has decorated the classroom with recent newspaper headlines, articles from news magazines, news features on congregational members, and prayer lists found in the church newsletter. These may be used for discussion right away, or later, depending on the nature of the biblical texts and the needs of the adults. The group reviews some basic Protestant principles of how to interpret the Bible and returns to the biblical passage, carefully thinking about its meaning(s) in today's world, especially in their lives and in their community and nation. At this time, the list made in step 1 is reviewed and modified based on new understandings; this initiates a discussion about the meaning of the biblical text.

Reflecting critically does not mean thinking with a negative or judgmental attitude; rather it means to discern, to make careful judgments. Reflecting critically pushes us to think about what we bring to our study; eventually it can lead to a radical reexamination of the way we act in our world. In the case of Bible study, critical reflection helps us to probe what we think about God, to examine the basic beliefs we use when we interpret the Bible, and to name the social-cultural context that has shaped our ideas. In this complex step of critical reflection, the tools of analysis, interpretation, assessment, and evaluation are added to the investigation of the previous step.

Adults are invited to ponder carefully and critically two sets of texts: the biblical texts and the "text of their lives." This latter text, the "life-text," includes the culture, the society, and the communities in which the learners live, as well as their individual lives. The focus on two texts facilitates the meeting of today's stories with yesterday's stories, and of God's stories with contemporary human stories.[8]

This step addresses adult learning needs by calling

upon adult experience and knowledge. Teachers treat lay adult learners with enough respect to teach them basic interpretive skills and to empower them to make connections with their own lives. The increasing levels of complexity in the study catch the learners' interests. The analysis of life-texts opens up the biblical text so that it can speak to the learner. Ideas and imaginations are sparked as biblical narratives encounter life narratives.

Empowering adults to interpret the Bible in a more complex manner affirms the Protestant tenet of faith that each member of the priesthood of all believers has the right and the duty to study and interpret the Bible. All Christians believe that those who follow Christ must be nurtured and equipped to grow in their knowledge of God and of God's call to them. Whether the goal of the study is to be converted, to find identity with the biblical communities, to hear God's call for active justice, or to grow closer to God by imitating Christ, this step deepens the learner's ability to hear God's word and respond accordingly.

The step of reflecting critically has three components: (1) using principles of interpretation relevant to this passage; (2) examining issues in the life-texts; (3) reflecting on the intersection of the first two. The first two components are ordered according to the interests of the class and the intuition of the teacher: either interpretation of the passage or examination of the life-texts can come first.

Using Principles of Biblical Interpretation

Once learners have explored the history, shape, and content of the text, they can begin thinking more carefully about what it means. This is the act that intimidates many of our churchgoers, especially with difficult or controversial passages. They wonder what to do with passages that contradict each other, with passages they do not like, and with passages they do not understand. Adults need at this point to be given some tools of interpretation. Four basic principles are used by most mainline denominations[9]:

1. Biblical texts must be understood within their historical and cultural context. In step 2, "Revisiting the Text," the question of context has been explored and has set the stage for understanding what issues the passage was addressing and why.

2. Biblical texts must be read within the framework of the larger text—the whole gospel, which is the good news of God's grace, love, and mercy. To lift a verse or small passage out of the larger biblical text is called "proof-texting." Placing this passage within the larger picture gives a more accurate understanding. This concern has been initiated in step 2, "Revisiting the Text." Employ additional questions, for example: Where else in the Bible is this subject addressed (or this story alluded to)? Are there references and quotes to other biblical verses in this passage? If so, what are they? Into what larger story or passage does this passage fit?

3. Jesus Christ is the center of our interpretation. What Jesus did and taught helps guide our interpretation and is "the bottom line." At the same time, we should recognize that not every text witnesses to Jesus. This key principle helps us to make judgments of what weight to give to different conflicting passages. We must ask, does this passage (or how does this passage) lead us to understand and live out the gospel of Jesus Christ, the gospel of God's goodness, love, and mercy?

4. God's Word is always calling us into God's future, God's new creation (Isa. 42:8–9, 65:17; Rom. 8:19–25). Although God's reign came more fully with Jesus Christ, God's new creation is not yet fully here. We are God's children and Christ's body on earth; therefore we work with God to transform the world to bring in God's new creation. For example, as a result of this principle, we eliminated slavery in the United States, working for God's kingdom, rather than taking literally biblical passages that approved of slavery (1 Tim. 6:1–2).

Examining the Life-texts of the Learners

In the first R step, "Remembering," the learners thought about what they already knew concerning the Bible passage being studied. In this step, they move away from the Bible text to thinking about their own lives and life in this world and this time. Creative teachers will find many ways to help adults identify important issues in their life-texts. One group can be invited to list local community issues, while another lists national and international ones. A third group can identify personal challenges and joys in the lives of church individuals. The whole group might work on all three areas. Newspapers, a videotaped news program from the night before, and information from the church newsletter or prayer list help adults identify major controversies, tragedies, and happy events in their lives. Alternatively, individuals may silently journal or think about their own issues and issues at a community/national level that concern them.

Interpreting the Bible as speaking both to individual and community is in accord with the traditional

Christian understanding of the Bible as the community book and a book that must be interpreted by and within the community of faith. Due to the American tendency to individualism, the teacher's role is to push learners to think beyond their own issues to those of the larger community and nation. At the same time, the teacher is a coinvestigator of these texts with the adults, bringing views and issues he sees as important, but insisting on the equal importance of the other learners' issues.

Reflecting on the Intersection of Bible and Life

After a separate analysis of the two texts, Bible and life, the connections between the two can begin to be made. A starting point is to have the class return to its lists and discussion from step 1, "Remembering," and compare its new understandings with the old. As the learners decide which items are still valid, which are not, and which need further exploration, discussion ensues about how the class is now interpreting the biblical text and what life issues it addresses. As some of the old items are discarded and new ones are added, "unlearning" and "relearning" occur. The teacher may spark discussion by drawing out those who disagree, by encouraging questions and varieties of opinions within a tolerant setting. This lively discussion encourages a variety of voices, which can increase interest and engagement by the adult learners.

Another tool to spark critical reflection is to introduce interpretations from other cultures and faiths. Jewish resources are very interesting when working in the Old Testament: translations and commentaries on Old Testament passages, rabbinic literature about these texts, and even Jewish folktales. Interpretations from other Christian groups can be challenging as well: for example, Ernesto Cardenal's the *Gospel in Solentiname* from Central America, and Clarence Jordan's fresh Cotton Patch translations from the American Old South.

Examples

A. *John 11:* The class discusses the headlines of yesterday's local paper. Of interest is the announcement by another denomination against women's ordination.[10] First Timothy 2:11–15 is quoted as a main reason for this decision. The participants then return to the biblical text of John 11 and are introduced to the four principles of interpretation; they note that they have been working on the first two in the step of "revisiting the text." In the process of revisiting the "remembering" list, they add other items that they have now noticed are important about the text. One of these items is that in the Gospel of John, Martha (a woman) is the one who (like Peter in the other Gospels) concludes that Jesus is the Messiah and "even now" could do whatever he wishes. The class begins to work on a response to the other denomination, such as a letter to the local paper, about why their denomination does ordain women.

Additional questions: In studying the John 11 passage, how has your understanding changed? What new insights have come to you? What do you think John was trying to communicate to us about Jesus and these disciples? What issues in your life does this text address? Are there social-political ones this speaks to? Why?

B. *The Pastoral Epistles:* The four interpretive principles are especially helpful as the group encounters 1 Timothy 2 and other controversial passages. They can affirm the purpose of the letters as a whole: to create a stable, loving church; to teach basic principles that oppose those proposed by some in that community (Holy Scripture is fundamental; matter as well as spirit is good; salvation comes through Jesus Christ). At the same time, they can look to Christ as the beginning of God's new creation and see that women were equally loved and allowed to lead. They can conclude that, even with these passages, slavery cannot be supported in light of God's reign.[11]

Reinterpreting

The class discussion flows into this step as the learners wrestle with how to interpret the text and what it means for them today. The teacher proposes that they compose a group sermon (very brief) about what the church should learn from this passage (How many points will we have? What are they?). Alternatively, she may ask willing persons to play the roles of characters in the story and improvise a scene.

Once we begin discussing the meaning of the text in light of our research and analysis, we are engaged in reinterpretation. The group working on John 11 above has already begun moving into this step.

Reinterpretation can be done analytically and imaginatively. Discussion continues on the meaning of the text, especially for our lives, building on the remembering step and the analysis in the reflecting step. One way to engage learners creatively in reinterpretation is to retell the passage in an imaginative manner as a short sermon, a story, a role-play, a skit, a letter or a pantomime. Learners can be paired with partners or divided into small groups, and each group can be asked to decide for itself the manner in which to retell and reinterpret the text. Reinterpretation done in a creative manner functions educationally to engage the adult learner at an affective, as well as cognitive, level; both mind and feelings are involved.

Storytelling is especially effective with biblical stories: parables can be retold in modern form (it is fascinating, for example, to see what modern type is chosen as the equivalent of a Samaritan); disciples can be interviewed by TV reporters; a therapist could be created to mediate between warring friends, siblings, or wives. Rewriting the text in today's language (for example, as a letter, an e-mail, an editorial, a poem) helps reinterpret other kinds of verses, such as exhortations or psalms.

The reinterpretation is colored by the biblical model of the Bible favored by the group. The conversion-model group, for example, may act out roles in which the characters are transformed by the event or write sermons calling for repentance. The justice-model group may invoke the need to act on God's call. The identity-model will note the unchanging nature of humankind and how God continues to work through us. The spiritual-growth-model may emphasize additional ways church members can grow in likeness to Christ. Each emphasis can be valid but should be named by the teacher. This naming may also help the learners understand where they differ in their interpretations. Hearing the different views opens up more meanings of the text. This plurality of meanings can allow God's Word to challenge and broaden us.

Examples

A. *John 11:* The John 11 text is one of the most dramatic stories in the Gospel of John. Jesus manifests his glory through raising a man from the dead.

His most faithful disciples, Martha and Mary, acknowledge him as Messiah. Thomas insists on sticking with his Teacher, even if it means dying with him. Key elements of who Jesus is are revealed: "I am the resurrection and the life," he says (v. 25). The implications for our faith in Jesus as Lord, and for our faithfulness as disciples, are many. Therefore discussion of the question, "What does this text teach me?" is important. Imaginative reinterpretation is also extremely effective here, I have found. The story can be told and retold from the point of view of the different characters: from the point of view of Thomas, of Martha, of Mary, of Lazarus, of other Jews present at the tomb, of the chief priests, and of Jesus. Each person depicting a character in the story begins with the words, "I am (name of character); let me tell you what just happened!"

B. *The Pastoral Epistles:* The pastorals can call forth many ways of engaging in reinterpretation: a debate on the ordination of women; a role-play in which a member of the church receiving these letters argues against slavery; prayers celebrating some key themes such as the importance of scripture and the goodness of matter; and so forth. Discussion may include questions that grow out of the different Bible study goals: How can we reclaim these letters for today? What are we called to repent from? What do we learn from this past community? What justice issues present themselves here? How can we imitate Christ more closely, according to these letters?

Responding

The group reviews what it has concluded are some major messages for today in this Bible study. They discuss what action is appropriate in light of the biblical text, and they covenant for group action. Alternatively, each person reflects in silence on his or her own behavior and journals a resolution for his or her life. Together they write a prayer of thanksgiving (which will be used in the church newsletter later on) and close the session by praying it together.

The first major challenge in the quest to move from study to action is to correlate our feelings and beliefs with our actions. Too often we listen to the Bible and, although it seems to move us deeply in our minds and hearts, we do not change our behavior or lifestyle. We churchgoing Christians know this: it is the human dilemma of sin. We know that James speaks truly when he asks, "What good is it, my brothers and sisters, if you say you have faith but do not have works?" (James 2:14). Living the faith is more difficult than talking about it.

The second challenge is that Christians do not necessarily agree on the right course of action in certain situations. While we can agree in general that murder and adultery are wrong, that anger should be curbed, and kindness and patience practiced, we disagree on when these might be allowed and, if so, how far. Is war, any war, or a certain war, murder? Is anger at injustice wrong? In what ways should we express anger? Is patience always the best way? Must I be poor and give up my middle-class lifestyle to be faithful? These questions are endless and, on the good side, are the source of many Christian ethical writings. On the bad side, they are a continuous source of division and war.

Response through action is essential for spiritual growth and transformation: action makes the text "part of us" and allows our encounter with it to transform our lives. In this step, the key question is,

"What does this text call us/me to be and to do?"
Two kinds of action are called for: (1) action through
behavior and ministry, and (2) action through ritual
(prayer and worship).

Behavior and Ministry

Action takes the concrete form of changing the
way we live, what we eat and buy, what we say and do.
Not all biblical texts demand this kind of action, but
many do. This response of action may seem obvious,
but it has traditionally been a difficult one for us. We
often leave our adult classes without discussing either
personal or political behavior. We are embarrassed to
discuss personal issues, and we are afraid of the pain
of political controversy. So we avoid both.

It takes a skillful teacher to help people reflect on
this kind of behavior and action. Many means can be
used to do this, means that will be determined by the
particular makeup of the group. The following list is
merely suggestive:

1. The teacher may discuss with the group why
   behavior and action are so difficult to talk
   about. The group may be able to devise strategies by which to talk about these issues and then
   to engage in action.
2. Silent time may be set aside for journaling on
   personal behavior. This is not intended to be
   shared or discussed.
3. The group may covenant together to engage in
   some common form of ministry as a result of
   the study. It may decide on a period of time in
   which to come up with a plan (such as six weeks,
   or three months, or after a study of Luke).
   Action might take the form of ministry within
   the congregation or mission and advocacy within
   the community. Bible study groups such as these

have, for example, written letters to advocate for paying dues to the United Nations, joined in political rallies and protests, started soup kitchens, engaged in prayer vigils, and organized volunteers to glean farmers' fields for the local food bank.[12]

4. Bible study can be started with a group already in active ministry, such as a group of deacons, that can covenant to add a Bible study (the starting point of Bible study does not need to be the Bible).

5. At the end of the class, participants can write down their decisions for personal and communal action and either keep them private or share them, for example, in prayer.

6. In discussion of the Bible passage, teachers need to poke and prod with thorny questions: "Does any of this have implications for our congregation, our nation?" "What are the implications for enhancing justice in this society?" These can be discussed if trust has been built up. If not, discussion with a trusted partner or silent prayer might be appropriate.

The discussion and decisions about appropriate action are always followed with the ritual action of prayer.

Ritual Action

Rituals are repetitive behavior by persons, often in the context of a believing community. Within the worship service, the rituals of prayer, of Bible readings, of sermons and creeds, and of sacraments have the educational function of teaching the biblical stories and transmitting Christian symbols. Through the cycles of weeks and years, the stories "are remembered not just verbally but through the body and thus doubly imprinted on [our] consciousness."[13] Liturgical ritual is what makes stories into sacred texts.

These rituals link the educational event, the Bible study, with the worship event, thus giving the study its purpose. Bible study without worship is ultimately meaningless, and worship without Bible study can lack depth and wholehearted participation.

In the step of "responding," these two events—education and worship—can be more purposely woven together. Not only should all study begin with prayer and invite the guidance of the Holy Spirit; every study should also end in a prayer response. The prayer response may have a variety of forms: silent prayer and personal offering by each participant; the group writing of a prayer or psalm that is prayed together; the offering of individual prayers by those who wish to do so; and so forth. Concluding responses can also include music and dance introduced by teacher or students. Some of these responses, such as written prayers, songs, or dances, may be used in Sunday morning worship; written material may be published in the church newsletter for the use of others. The response of prayer closes the Bible study but opens the individual and the group to further guidance by the Holy Spirit.

Examples

A. *John 11:* After reinterpreting the John 11 passage with a multitude of stories, the group may be elated but tired. At this time, some silent reflection on questions of action is appropriate: "What does this story call me to be and do? How will I change? I now pledge myself to . . ." After a solid time of silence, the group can join in prayer, or create a prayer, line by line, and say it in unison. Women's groups, excited by the strong role of Martha, sometimes celebrate Martha and the implications of her actions for their own discipleship. Other groups reconsider Thomas and his faithfulness as a guide for their lives as disciples.

B. *Pastoral Epistles:* These epistles have many implications for actions. The group may act to counter the use of the texts on women and slaves to oppress African Americans and women. The learners may propose ways to use the epistles to inspire their congregation to repent from argument and dissension and find solidarity of purpose with tolerance and love. They may wish to write a prayer of repentance for the church for the effect of these texts and a prayer of celebration for God's new creation begun in Jesus Christ, a creation in which "there is no longer Jew or Greek, there is no longer slave or free, there is no longer male and female: for all of you are one in Christ Jesus" (Gal. 3:28).

Conclusion

The encounter of the biblical text and the text of our lives within the community of faith is an occasion for God's revelation. This encounter, therefore, can be powerful, exciting, disturbing, tiring, and energizing, all at once. Not every encounter will be transformative. The day comes, however, when some insight, some story, or some litany will stir the heart and the mind and direct the will in a new way. Although God is certainly able to work in a number of ways to move and convert us, we as teachers need to be faithful to an educational process that can engage adults in heart, mind, and will.

The five R steps will interest and educate adults, although perhaps in different ways, whatever the model of the Bible and educational goal the group favors. This five Rs model is to be used as a blueprint and modified by the educator. New models can be constructed by utilizing the educational dimensions that underlie this model. These dimensions—storytelling and imagination, critical-analytical reflection, and action—are described in the next chapter.

The Five Rs Model

A Study of John 11

1. Remembering

What do you remember about this story? List stereotypes of Mary, Martha, Lazarus, and Jesus. Do you remember any verses?

2. Revisiting the Text

Behind-the-text historical questions: Who wrote this? When, where, and why? Use Bible research tools such as concordances, atlases, dictionaries, and commentaries (print and/or computer programs).

In-the-text literary questions: How do key words, players, structure, characters all function?

What do you think John was trying to communicate to us about Jesus and about these disciples?

3. Reflecting Critically

Using silent reflection, sharing with a neighbor, reviewing the four principles of interpretation, address these questions:

1. In studying the John 11 passage, how was your understanding changed? What new insights have come to you?
2. What issues in your life does this text address? Are there social-political ones this speaks to? Why?

4. Reinterpreting

Listen to a tape recreating a character; or discuss some art about this scene.

In groups, retell the story from the point of view of Thomas, Mary, Martha, Lazarus, a Jew who questioned, a Jewish priest.

5. Responding

What does this call me to do? What ministry does it call our congregation to? Write a few words of commitment for yourself on paper. Discuss possible actions a congregational or community group could take.

Group litany: create a prayer to God . . . and then pray this prayer.

Chapter Four

The Three Primary Colors of Bible Study

The Bible study leaders of several churches were meeting. Several of them shared curriculum they liked and disliked. One was excited by the five Rs model. Finally, one who had been listening with an increasing frown on his face joined in: "I don't like most published curriculums, and we can't afford the most popular ones. I'm also not good at following a model step by step. I just want a general guide so that I can build my own study and know that I am doing the right thing!"

In the previous chapter, we have looked at the steps the artist/teacher can take to create a canvas that illuminates the Bible for the adult learners. The five Rs offer a guide to which colors might be used, combined with hints on technique and brush strokes. The creative artist, however, often wishes to find new techniques and steps and to mix the colors in different and varied ways. The painter then explores the basic ingredients of her medium, learning what they are, how they work, and playing with new ways to use them. In the same manner, this chapter offers the Bible teacher some understanding of the basic educational ingredients that should be used to paint the Bible study canvas. These educational elements are the primary *colors* of sound Bible study.

Just as the artist mixes red, yellow, and blue in an infinite variety of ways to create, so can the creative teacher put together in many ways three primary educational elements to create an interesting, effective, and faithful plan for study with adults. The artist/teacher can use them as he develops his own plan, or as he evaluates already published curriculum. They are the educational elements that underlie the five Rs model and could be used to form other patterns. These elements are: (1) disciplined imagination and story, (2) critical-analytical reflection, and (3) action through ritual and ministry.

Three educational acts lie at the heart of each of these elements of Bible study. Disciplined imagination calls for the educational mode of "play." Critical-analytical reflection centers on "problem-posing dialogue" as the central teaching-learning method. Finally, ritual and action evoke the educational act we could call "performance."[1]

Storytelling and Disciplined Imagination

In a study of 2 Samuel 12, the teacher divides the class into two groups, naming one group "Nathan" and the other "David." The Nathan group reads 2 Samuel 12:1–15 silently, while the David group silently reads 2 Samuel 11, the story of Bathsheba and Uriah, which precedes the Nathan story. The Nathan group then prepares quickly to present Nathan's speech (in first person) to "David" (the group). After the presentation, the David group caucuses and decides how to respond. After their response, the group goes back to the story to read what David actually did in response to Nathan.

Storytelling and other acts of disciplined imagination are essential to the study of the Bible. This "color" of Bible study is the aesthetic dimension, a dimension that appeals strongly to our affective, feeling side and also engages our intellect, weaving together mind and emotion to further learning and knowledge. Faith is the kind of knowledge that especially engages both mind and feeling. Faith is powered by images, symbols, rituals, and stories that shape how we make ultimate sense of our lives, giving us vision and purpose and requiring imagination.[2]

Imagination, therefore, is crucial to developing faith. While imagination is important in conceptual and critical thought, it is especially present in the arts, in story, poetry, song, and dance. In this chapter we engage in a brief exploration of how this "color" of disciplined imagination functions and of ways in which the teacher can utilize it in Bible study.

A student approached the Teacher with a question. "When Jesus told the man to sell all that he had and give it to the poor, did he mean that we must get rid of everything?"

The Teacher answered with a story: "Once there was a man who listened to the Scripture. One day he heard Jesus quoted as saying to the rich man, 'Go! Sell all that you have, give to the poor, and you will have riches in heaven, and come follow me.'

"The man stiffened. This was a word to him, for he, like the rich man, was seeking salvation. First, he sold his car. After he gave the money away, he again listened, and heard Jesus say, 'Sell all!'

"Next he sold his house. After he gave the money away he listened again, and heard Jesus say, 'Sell all!'

"All that he had left was his Bible, which he sold for a few dollars. When he gave the money away, he again listened. This time he heard nothing."

The student said, "Teacher, I don't understand this story. Why did the man hear nothing?"

The Teacher answered, "He heard nothing because he sold the one thing that brought him the voice of God. We are not asked to rid ourselves of those things that draw us close to the heart of God. Jesus told the man to sell everything because his possessions were an idol. We must rid ourselves of whatever stands in the way of God. Now you must decide whether the things you own bring you close or separate you from God."[3]

The idea of storytelling and disciplined imagination as an important part of Bible study has ancient and sound roots in Jewish interpretations of the Hebrew scriptures called midrash.[4] Midrash is work done by the rabbis (and early Christian teachers) to explain the biblical texts.[5] Midrash has developed in a variety of forms, one of which is commentary in the form of story. The teacher may add into the retelling of the story such elements as hymns, prayers, speeches, and narrative sections. The goal, to show "the eternal relevance of biblical truth," is grounded in the traditional conviction "that the Bible can be made to speak to the present day."[6]

This process of "disciplined imagination" is open-ended, "simultaneously serious and playful, imaginative, metaphoric."[7] Our imaginative play with biblical texts will be built on these basic understandings: (1) our goal as teachers is to help our students hear God's truth with their whole heart; (2) we teachers are grounded in and have a keen knowledge of the whole of the Bible; (3) we teachers are grounded in and have a keen knowledge of our community and our world.

Many teachers worry that by using imagination in

thinking about God and listening to biblical texts, they risk falling on the wrong interpretation. Yet scholars agree that there is no one final interpretation of the text. In the imaginative act of interpretation, what is important is not "reading into" but "reading out of" the text, states the author of *The Gospel According to Peanuts*. He points out that it is impossible to tell if the author and the reader's vision coincide exactly. More to the point is what we hear in the text and whether the word that we hear brings salvation.[8] God's Spirit is free and strong enough to work through wide varieties of interpretation.

We are so concerned with orthodoxy and being right that we try to make our God a tame, safe God. But our God can work to save us through many interpretations. A Jewish folktale from eastern Europe illustrates the point.

A cruel king declared that he would put all the Jews to death unless one person could win a silent duel with him. A simple cobbler came forward to engage the king. The king began the duel by raising his forefinger. The cobbler pointed straight down.

The king's eyes widened in surprise. He thrust two fingers at the little cobbler. The cobbler thrust one finger at the king.

The king thrust out his whole hand at the Jew. The cobbler held up his fist.

Frowning, the king held up a bottle of red wine. Shrugging, the cobbler took a piece of white cheese out of his pocket.

"Enough!" cried the king. "You have won—name your reward."

"I wish for nothing for me, your Majesty. I only want your promise that you will never bother the Jews again."

"Agreed," muttered the king.

After the cobbler had left, the king's puzzled attendants asked what the silent duel had meant.

"*When I pointed up,*" *the king told them,* "*I was saying that the Jews were as many as the stars. The cobbler pointed down, answering that they were as the grains of sand.*

"*When I pointed with two fingers, I was saying there are two gods, one of good, one of evil. When he pointed with only one finger, he was saying there is only one God.*

"*My third gesture, with my whole hand, meant that the Jews are scattered all over the world. His fist said that the Jews are still united.*

"*My last gesture, holding up the wine, said his sins were red as wine. He replied that no, they were white as cheese.*"

Meanwhile, though, the cobbler was explaining the duel in a very different way to his friends.

"*Well, first he pointed up to tell me he wanted to hang me. So I pointed down, telling him to go to the devil!*

"*Then he tried to poke out my eyes with his two fingers, so I pointed back, telling him it would be an eye for an eye!*

"*That got him really mad. He tried to slap me with his whole hand, so I warned him with my fist not to try it!*

"*Now the king was scared of me. He offered me a drink of wine. What could I do but be polite and offer him some cheese? And that's when he knew I had won.*" *The cobbler shrugged.* "*It was easy!*"[9]

What is it about stories and poetry and song and art that captures and enthralls us? What makes them "work"? Volumes have been written on the inner workings of art in its various forms. More and more theologians have acknowledged the power of stories and images in shaping our faith. The current understandings can be summarized in five key points.

1. *Disciplined imagination works holistically on mind and feeling, through images, symbols, and metaphors.* The Bible is brimming with the poems, stories,

metaphors, symbols, dreams, and images of religious experience. This language functions first to draw us in and respond. Story and art help us listen to the text as a Thou; we must become involved.[10] With that involvement we, and our world, become something new. Secondly, this imaginative language puts religious experience into words using stories and metaphors: "The Holy Spirit descended upon him in bodily form like a dove." (Luke 3:22). "I was traveling to Damascus . . . when at midday along the road . . . I saw a light from heaven. . . . I heard a voice saying to me in the Hebrew language, 'Saul, Saul, why are you persecuting me?'" (Acts 26:12–14). At the same time these stories and images allow us to begin the act of reflection through which theological concepts such as "grace," "salvation," and "sin" are understood.

2. *Disciplined imagination works as a bridge to nature, to our culture, and to our roots.* Whether it is a poem such as e.e. cummings's "I thank you God for most this amazing day"; or the Navajo chant of the Beauty Way, "In beauty I walk, beauty above me, beauty before me . . ."; or the song of the psalmist, "You stretch out the heavens like a tent, /you set the beams of your chambers on the waters, /you make the clouds your chariot, /you ride on the wings of the wind . . ." (Ps. 104:2–3)—in all these aesthetic forms we are reunited with the natural environment. We are invited to new levels of appreciation and sometimes even awe.[11]

In a similar manner, stories and art bind us to our culture and to our own roots.[12] One of the ways stories and art shape identity and faith is that they speak in the contemporary language of the day. They translate long-lasting truths into images and symbols that can be used by the current generation. Thus they weave together tradition and contemporary culture. Just as missionaries must learn the language of the new country to which they are going, so we can use art to acquaint us with the contemporary world. We can then use it to translate the gospel into contemporary language.[13]

3. *Disciplined imagination can disturb and shock.* An important film of the 1990s was Stephen Spielberg's *Schindler's List.* This story is about a slightly sleazy German entrepreneur in Nazi Germany who winds up saving more than a thousand Jews from annihilation in death camps. The movie has been extremely popular and has won many awards. Some people, however, voiced doubts about going to see it. Many of us who did go admitted that we did so somewhat reluctantly, going out of duty to remember again the pain of the Holocaust so that it might not ever happen again. We knew that to remember this story would be shocking and disturbing. Yet the picture was both more hopeful and affirming while at the same time more disturbing than we expected. It raised so many questions about human nature and human motivation, about human depravity and human goodness, about the role of the individual and the role of the community. It led us into the deepest mysteries of life—good and evil, life and death, God and humanity—offering no simple answers, only the complexity of the story.

Imagination "involves, disturbs, and challenges" us in ways that analytical thinking often does not.[14] It helps us delve into the mysteries of life and involves us in ideas that are simultaneously deeply painful and joyful, shocking and comforting, despairing and hopeful. Because imagination pushes us emotionally and intellectually further into the complex mysteries of life we can be led to repentance and conversion.

4. *Disciplined imagination provides vision, hope, and healing.*

Mary stood weeping outside the tomb. . . . "They have taken away my Lord, and I do not know where they have laid him." When she had said this, she turned around and saw Jesus standing there, but she did not know that it was Jesus. Jesus said to her, "Woman, why are you weeping? Whom are you looking for?" Supposing him to be the gardener, she said to him, "Sir, if you have carried him away, tell me where you have laid him, and I will take him away." Jesus said to her, "Mary!" She turned and said to him in Hebrew, "Rabbouni!" (which means Teacher). Jesus said to her, "Do not hold on to me, because I have not yet ascended to the Father. But go to my brothers and say to them, 'I am ascending to my Father and your Father, to my God and your God.' Mary Magdalene went and announced to the disciples, "I have seen the Lord"; and she told them that he had said these things to her. (John 20:11–18)

No story matches this one, the core story of our faith, for providing vision, hope, and healing. And God works through many other stories as well, biblical stories and nonbiblical stories. We can distinguish between false stories and true stories. One scholar complains that most television stories are not true. "A true story must either help us to see the world as it is or show what it can become."[15]

The vision that true stories provide is not always of the great meanings of life and death. They may carry simple moral understandings of kindness and cruelty, right and wrong, faithfulness and infidelity. They may teach about pride coming before a fall, or that all that glitters is not gold, or not to count chickens before they hatch. They may also look under the surface to the true nature of things: the bumbling younger "idiot" son or daughter turns out to be wise in kindness and courtesy and thereby wins the love of the prince or princess. The quick, proud rabbit can lose a race with a patient turtle. Stories provide hope and vision about what is true and right and ultimately beautiful. This wisdom brings hope and healing to the spirit and soul.

5. *Disciplined imagination links us to all humankind.* "To be a person is to have a story." And to hear someone else's story is in part to hear our own, for "every story is our story."[16] Stories, paintings, poems, and all forms of art link us to other individuals, to other communities, to other cultures, to other times. They help us to experience what those people experience. They allow us to discover our common humanity, joys, and sufferings.

One of the important ways in which stories and other art bind us with humanity is through universal archetypes or images. These are symbols and images, often found in dreams and visions, that crop up again and again across time and space.[17] Yet symbols can mean different things in different cultures. The dragon, for example, is a symbol of power, strength, and royalty in many Asian cultures, while in Europe it has long represented evil and the dark side of life. In the East, the color white has symbolized death, whereas for the West it has meant purity. Sometimes, to listen truly to story or art, we will need to analyze and revisit symbols and images in light of the culture producing them.

In hearing the story of another's pain and suffering, we can name our pain and suffering. In listening to stories of joy and hope, we can find joy and hope in our lives. Furthermore, in listening to the other's story, we discover that the other is not so very different from us after all. We are all creatures together, sons of Adam and daughters of Eve, which, as Aslan reminds us, is enough to bow the head of the mightiest ruler and raise the pride of the lowest peasant.[18]

Teaching Methods

> Like gentle jewels
> Gem bright images catch my mind
> Changing my world.

The central educational process for disciplined imagination is play. Anyone who watches children play knows that play is very serious business. It involves singing, drama, make-believe, role playing, nonverbal language, dance and movement, and art. The act of playing with the Bible is not an act of irreverence but of joy: it is to dance around the sanctuary carrying the Torah, the Word of God, as the Hasidic Jews do in the synagogue. The act of playing with the Bible calls for *story time*, with its quiet listening, *rest time* to meditate in silence, *creation time*, to paint and color and write poetry and more stories, *drama time* to act and role play, and *sharing time*, to tell our stories.

In a study of the Gospel of John, one of my classes began by using some critical-analytical tools. With this background we returned to hear the story. Each member of the group chose a character in this gospel and told his or her story in first person. We arranged people in the order that they appear in the John narrative. Some important characters, such as Nicodemus, were chosen by two members, some were not chosen at all. We then each told "our" story. "I am Mary of Nazareth, mother of Jesus. My son had been restless for months. I knew it was time for him to step out and declare himself, but he still kept doing nothing. Then we went to this wedding . . ." "I am Nicodemus. Some say that I sneaked in to see Jesus at night because I was afraid . . ." "I don't know why the church has not remembered my name. I am the Samaritan woman he talked to on that fateful day . . ." and so on to the end of the story. In this particular group, one of the stories was told by Thomas the Twin's twin. "My brother always did have to have proof for everything, but he was forever loyal . . ." By the end of the stories, we were stunned into silence. The strength of these stories was overwhelming. We had heard the gospel.

Story time is the act of listening to the story. It may also involve listening to poems and hymns or attending to paintings, icons, or other aesthetic material. There are many ways to do this. Sometimes we start with the text and have someone read the story out loud. It helps to have everyone else close their eyes and listen. Sometimes we can start with someone else's version of the same story. I often use a tape in which Hagar tells her story: "My name is Hagar, black Hagar. . . . My father sold me to the old Abraham . . ."[19] Sometimes we listen to a folktale or another (sometimes subversive) version of a biblical story. Books are being published that retell the stories of biblical women in both prose and poetry, often with a critical bite.

A favorite of mine is Ursula LeGuin's brief story "She Unnames Them," in which Eve frees all the animals of the names Adam gave them (some animals do not want to be unnamed, especially pet dogs and birds; and cats maintain that they had only the secret names they had given themselves).[20] Literature, from the classics to science fiction and mysteries, can be read together and discussed. Movies, popular and classical music, TV shows, cartoons, even comic books, can be shared. Paintings and icons can be studied. We can listen for biblical themes or religious ideals. Then we can return to the biblical texts.

Another way to tell biblical stories is for adults in the class to read and study the text and then retell the story to the class in the first person as described in the example above.[21] This seemingly simple exercise is a central tool of *drama time* and seems to be extremely effective. It is another creative form of learning and telling the story. Some groups bring video cameras to film the final storytelling. Some groups retell the stories in modern form.

This retelling works well with parables. A group led by a young adult with cerebral palsy retold and enacted the parable of the good Samaritan, with the Samaritan being a disabled person like himself. We all heard the parable in a new way, and we learned something about what his world is like for him.

Role-playing is also a quick way to include a little drama. People can role-play the Esau-Jacob story or start by role-playing the conflict between two siblings in their lives.[22] Songs and dances have also been created, celebrating biblical events and persons.

Storytelling and drama often mix with *creation time*, an educational tool that is especially effective in retreat settings where a leisurely span of time is available. Participants write poems or psalms together, or they use crayons and clay to draw and sculpt.[23] They know that this art is that of novices; the pleasure and the learning is in the act of creation which expresses ideas and feelings evoked by the story. Cloth banner making, finger paints, modeling clay, and watercolors can all be employed. Adults find themselves working creatively together as a group, or quietly as individuals, expressing in new ways what the biblical stories and materials mean to them. This creativity helps the biblical material work more deeply within the psyche and soul. And it is a lot of fun.

Woven throughout is *sharing time*. Stories and art evoke our own stories. Women's groups have long understood this need to wander into personal story. The members of women's groups have listened tolerantly to many a story. This can drive goal-oriented teachers crazy. It is important to recognize, however, that this listening is "hearing the person into speech"[24] and helping them to connect to their faith, their group, and the larger story.[25] God works in us to create and change our story, and in telling that story we can recognize God at work in our lives.

The hearing brought by these activities eventually calls for silence. This *rest time* is a time of quiet meditation and thought. In the noisy, busy world of today, a quiet time in which to think is a luxury. It is also a necessity. It allows the hearing to sink in, the thoughts and feelings to rise up like bubbles in a placid lake. Silence is a necessary component of education, a crucial element in listening, thinking, and dialoguing.

Many Bible study curricula are filled with creative ways to play with the biblical stories and engage in the color of disciplined imagination. These ideas form a modern type of midrash: retelling the stories, creating new stories, tying them into our personal stories, acting and dancing and illustrating them. Such imaginative education speaks to adults at all different levels of understanding and knowledge. Storytelling and disciplined imagination are especially appealing to adults who have been unchurched and are intimidated by the Bible. By beginning with biblical stories, they can begin to connect with biblical texts in an enjoyable, interesting, yet challenging way.

Critical-Analytical Reflection

In their study of the David cycle, in 1 and 2 Samuel, the class wanted to know more about the background of the stories which they had been reading and dramatizing. Who wrote them, when, and why? Why did some texts seem to put the king in a good light and some in a bad one? How did the geography and the culture of the area and historical era come into play? The class compiled a list of questions. When they arrived at the next session, their tables were covered with Bible atlases, dictionaries, concordances, and commentaries—some of the most interesting-looking ones had come from the older children's classrooms. Different people chose different questions to research, chose their tools (guided by the teacher), and reported back to the class. In a following session, they listed themes raised by these stories (adultery, vengeance, rape, youthful rebellion, etc.) and began a discussion about similar themes in their own community.

A second primary color necessary for the artist/ teacher is the educational element of critical-analytical reflection. As we have seen in chapter 3, *critical* is used here in the scholarly sense, based on its Greek root, "to discern." Critical reflection does not mean thinking with a negative attitude. Biblical criticism is a "process through which discerning judgments are made."[26] It calls for analyzing and reflecting on the text. This kind of reflection has been prized in the history of biblical study.

Yet teachers and ministers seem to find it difficult to teach the Bible in an analytical, critical manner.

The first problem is the gap between church professionals and laity. For most of this century, the majority of ministers and Christian educators have received training in the use of historical-critical tools. For the most part, however, the laity in our congregations have not been taught even the simplest of these tools. In my experience, teachers worry that using historical-critical tools will, at best, bore their adult students, and at worst, shake their faith. This lack of lay training has undermined the foundational tenet of the Protestant Reformation, which insists on the right and duty of every Christian to read and interpret the Bible. It has encouraged the laity to see teachers and the clergy as professional experts, gurus of biblical wisdom, rather than as guides for their own explorations of the Bible. Furthermore, critical-analytical tools are perceived as scholars' tools, not easily accessible to teachers or laypeople. As a result, teachers often neither use nor teach the use of traditional critical tools.

Yet critical-analytical tools and skills offer us help in hearing the biblical text in new or clearer ways. Critical-analytical exploration opens up one way to hear God's word and to know the truth. The interpretation guided solely by personal feelings and stories can risk reinforcing our human biases and keep us from hearing God's truth. A partnership of critical-analytical reflection and of personal and communal stories creates a more faithful act of interpretation.[27]

The volunteer teacher and the ordinary churchgoer can learn some of these basic critical skills. As we have seen in chapter 3's model, adults can be taught to ask some basic analytical questions and to use some of the scholar's tools, such as atlases, concordances, Bible dictionaries, and commentaries. In my experience, adults are grateful, interested, and empowered by teaching that offers them these proficiencies.

Critical-analytical reflection goes further than the use of historical-critical tools, however. The goal of critical reflection is to move beyond knowledge to understanding and finally wisdom.[28] Such critical thinking challenges learners to engage with thought that is uncomfortable, unexpected, and even dissonant. This reflection can foster significant personal transformation.[29]

In previous chapters we noted that reflection is the act of thinking something over, using tools of analysis, assessment, and evaluation, and is facilitated by being involved in "layers of reflection." In other words, critical reflection involves thinking again and again about the subject. Additional layers of reflection are to be more than simple repetition; they add a probing into why and how we think and see in certain ways. In the case of Bible study, critical reflection helps us to analyze and assess our theological assumptions and methods (as in chapter 1), and to name the social-cultural context that has shaped them.

Problem-posing dialogue is the foundational educational method for critical-analytical investigation.[30] Critical-analytical reflection using the educational method of problem-posing dialogue allows adults to investigate various interpretations of the biblical text and search for truth together with others in the community of faith. Guided by the Holy Spirit, the search for truth places the learners into dialogue with a variety of understandings of the biblical texts: understandings growing from the use of modern historical-critical tools; interpretations by earlier Christians such as Augustine, Calvin, Luther, and Wesley; and interpretations from different voices in today's world, such as women, the poor, and Christians of other countries.

The educational method of problem-posing dialogue focuses also on a second kind of dialogue: one between the text of the Bible and the text of our contemporary lives. What problems arise in our society, our local communities, and our individual lives? What problems are addressed in the biblical texts being studied? What do we learn as we bring these two texts into dialogue about what God is doing and desiring us to do in today's world? To begin this dialogue, analysis is brought to the two basic texts being studied: the Bible and our lives.

Critical Reflection on the Biblical Text

The goal of critical reflection on the biblical text is to listen to the biblical text and to hear its voice afresh, so that the event that we call revelation, in which we come to know God and ourselves better, can occur. The first step of critical reflection is to develop our listening skills.[31] The second step is to be able to name meaningful issues growing out of this listening. We must also remember that the acts of both listening and naming are interpretive acts, set within a specific contemporary context.

In steps 2 and 3 of the five Rs model, "Revisiting the Text" and "Reflecting Critically," we have reviewed much of what this educational element of Bible study entails. Critical-analytical reflection can be built into Bible study in a variety of ways. The discussion below briefly describes the essential components so that artist/teachers can use them as they wish. This element of Bible study, however, is crucial for an effective and faithful curriculum and must not be omitted.

1. *Historical-critical questions:* The goal of biblical "criticism" is to listen to the text through the lens of certain historical-context and literary questions. Different questions lead to the use of different tools. We are thus reminded again that part of Bible study is learning which questions to ask and why certain questions are more helpful at certain times than others.

Behind-the-text questions: The simple "w" questions—who, what, when, where, and why—can serve as guides. Who wrote the text? Who was the audience? When and where was it written (it may have been written long after the period of time it reflects and in a different land)? Does it reflect the period it writes about accurately? What does it emphasize or leave out from that period? Why was the author writing it?

In-the-text questions: As described in chapter 3, *how* the text is written matters a great deal for its meaning. Every word and shape of phrase, each sequence of events, description of characters and settings, the use of wordplay and puns, rhythms and rhymes, structure of an argument—all of these are purposefully structured to give meaning and feeling to the story, the poem, or the exposition of an idea. The in-text questions look at the *what* and *how* questions: What kind of a writing is it—story, letter, poem, oracle, exhortation? How does this text (story, poem, and the like) work? How has the writer repeated words or used a unique one? What is the emphasis, the climax, the key point? A study of biblical stories raises questions about plot, character, action, and dialogue.

In order to research these behind-the-text and in-the-text questions, teachers and students can explore the traditional tools used by pastors: different translations of the passage from different Bibles, concordances, atlases, Bible dictionaries, Bible encyclopedias, the introductions and the notes in study Bibles, and certain Bible commentaries.[32] As stated earlier, adults are often charmed by the materials printed for youth, especially atlases, dictionaries, and encyclopedias, which are filled with colorful pictures of Roman armor, Bible land plants, animals, foods, and furniture, and simple maps.

2. *Interpretive questions:* Questions of interpretation come up even as the historical questions are explored. Teachers can begin by using chapter 1 as a guide for identifying models of interpretation that are present among the adults in the class. Is the stress on a holy God and sinful humanity drowning out the learner who insists on God's call for justice for the poor? Is the sin of humanity unmentioned by a group intent on developing a close, nurturing relationship with God? Such questions may help identify what is guiding people's interpretations.

I have also described four basic principles of biblical interpretation in chapter 3. These principles are helpful to review and use as interpretive issues arise. They are especially important as the biblical text is brought into dialogue with themes from contemporary life. They serve as guides as we make judgments about the validity of other interpretations of the biblical text being studied.

1. Biblical texts must be understood within their historical and cultural context.
2. Biblical texts must be read within the framework of the larger text—the whole gospel, which is the good news of God's grace, love, and mercy.

3. Jesus Christ is at the center of our interpretation.
4. God's Word is always calling us into God's future, God's new creation.

These four principles, explained in detail in chapter 3, are grounded in an understanding that biblical interpretation must take place with the guidance of the Holy Spirit. Since we Christians understand the Spirit to be present when we gather in faithful, covenant community, we also believe that the Bible must be studied in this community, not apart from it. Even when we study it alone, we dialogue with our brothers and sisters who are in a covenant relationship with God.

Critical-Analytical Reflection on Life-Texts

American educators have found a variety of educational techniques to help adults investigate their own society and their personal role in it. One way is for the teacher to name a theme, such as racism, and invite the students to write about or share a memory of having encountered racism.[33] Another assignment said, "Please bring a list of words that seem to you to be keys to areas of knowledge or life that you want to open up; then group these words in any way they seem to fit together to you." The words were gathered and arranged and rearranged by students and teachers. The result was two lists, one "good" group and one "bad" group (as defined by the students). The group the students felt badly about included things they felt they had no power over: government, education, mind, environment; these were opposed to the "good" things that they could control: emotion, belief, art, love, God, music, and so on. The importance of generating themes was not to lay out themes by themselves, but to discuss "the students' relation to those themes."[34]

Adult learning theory, as summarized in chapter 2, has shown us that study in the abstract tends to be of less interest to adults in this society. They want to see the immediate relevance of their learning and to learn out of the richness of their personal experience. They hope that through learning their practical needs will be met. The big question for educators and pastors often is, "How do I help adults make the connection between their lives and the Bible?"

To meet this goal, the teacher must know and understand the lives of the students. Most church professionals do. They understand the stress of life in this society: lack of time, scattered families, shrinking income, the isolation of single people, the increase in violence and fear, numbing materialism, the increase in prejudice and extremist rhetoric, the AIDS epidemic. They can name the blessings of living in the United States and Canada: fairly comfortable lifestyles, good doctors, clean water, political freedoms, technological advancements.

The goal of critical-analytical thinking of self and society is to help adults reflect on the realities with which they live, both interior and exterior, psychological and social-cultural. The goal, furthermore, is to push deeper and bring out assumptions and values that shape the way we see our lives. This reflection can help us eventually to think about how to bring the world of the biblical text into our world.

Critical-analytical reflection on self and society involves, in a sense, helping adults become anthropologists who can step back and take a long look at themselves and their culture somewhat objectively. This long look is aided by parallel reflection on the biblical passages that they are studying. The role of the teacher is to stimulate this thinking through the presentation of strategies, questions, and materials. One helpful method is to investigate major social and psychological themes that dominate contemporary life. These themes may be ones identified together by learners and teachers. They may also grow out of the biblical material or be introduced by the teacher or a student.[35]

Themes need to grow out of dialogue among students and teachers, but they can be arrived at in different ways. I propose three simple starting points that can spark this reflection within Bible study. Teachers may think of others as they work with this approach. No starting point is "better" than another. The kind of group being taught and the style of the teacher will determine which one to use.

1. *Student-generated themes:* Students are asked to list key words or themes that affect or worry them. These words could be nouns or verbs. They should convey some of the reality of living in their country, town, and county at this time in history and/or the anxieties or the joys about their work and relationships. These words can be tabulated and shared with the group. Discussion includes what these words mean in the lives of the adults in the group.

Student-generated words and themes can be encouraged by bringing in newspapers, weekly periodicals, tabloids, brief articles on contemporary society, and so on. Other catalysts can be

- to provide open-ended sentences for individuals to finish ("What worries me the most about my society is . . ." "What I find most difficult/easy to do in my everyday life is . . .");
- to provide quiet time to write down a critical incident;

- to write a poem such as a haiku or cinquain, or to think privately about life's challenges.

2. *Teacher-generated themes:* Teacher-generated themes need to come after careful listening to the students. They should be critiqued and discussed and modified in student discussion. However, teachers can be important initiators, especially in adult groups dominated by people who dislike being asked to produce.

Teachers can bring in suggested themes they have culled from local newspapers and other public information media. They can introduce themes they have been studying in current literature or give a brief lecture. Some important themes playing themselves out in today's society might be

- unity and diversity (one culture, many subcultures, multiculturalism);
- freedom of speech and its limits (insults and verbal abuse; pornography);
- personal freedom and social responsibility (for example, limits of gun ownership and problems of violence);
- the women's movement and the men's movement;
- materialism and spirituality.

One way to spark lively discussion is to use "loaded" words that are often stereotyped. The group then discusses the range and limits of those words. An example is *feminism.* People define this word very differently. The difference is most apparent among generations. A debate over this word raises many issues, themes, and ideas that can be critically pursued.

3. *Bible-generated themes:* The Bible is full of themes that speak to human experience. Themes of

rich and poor, freedom and oppression, abundant life and poor lives, family and community, and so forth can be useful starting points for a discussion of modern life as well. The danger is to move too quickly into the biblical world and away from analysis of contemporary life and context of the students.

Additional Layers of Reflection

Additional interpretations can come from the more distant historical past, the recent (within living memory) past, or the present. They can come from communities on this continent and around the world. Thus, for example, a teacher could bring the Barmen Confession written in Nazi Germany in 1934, as an example of interpretation of what the Lordship of Jesus Christ means, especially as we relate to secular governments. Cardenal's *The Gospel in Solentiname* provides provocative interpretations of the Bible by poor peasants in Nicaragua. Commentaries by Calvin, Luther, Barth, and other important Protestant theologians can offer segments of interpretation to be shared. Writings by church fathers and mothers and by medieval mystics all contribute interpretations within the Christian tradition.

We have seen that thinking again and again about a subject, asking more questions, pushing to think about presuppositions, describing assumptions and definitions of words and issues can create layers of reflection that help learners progress from knowledge to understanding. However, for transformation to occur, people often need challenge, difference, and the unexpected.

How can we teachers provide this dimension? This is where sensitivity to the learners, personal experience, and creativity come into play. One important method is to bring alternate interpretations of the biblical passage to the group. This act introduces voices of other Christian communities. Introducing other interpretations is an act of dialogue, not the act of knocking over a weak argument. Thus, information about the context in which these interpretations were made (for example, poverty in Latin America, or the killing of Christians in Indonesia) is essential in order for these interpretations to be understood as valid expressions of Christian faith.

Dialogue with these interesting and challenging interpretive communities may shock and shake or comfort and reassure. They will push learners to think more profoundly. They offer an opening for that "aha!" moment, for the unexpected. This work, however, is ultimately that of the Holy Spirit, ever calling us to conversion and sanctification.

Intersecting the Two Sets of Texts

The starting point for putting together these two sets of texts is not important and depends on what is appropriate to the groups of learners and the texts. Because the Bible is the subject of study, we often start there. But we are not obligated to do so. We may choose instead to start with some critical reflection on self and society. This reflection may lead us to choose certain biblical texts to study. We listen carefully to the biblical text itself, utilizing the critical tools described above. Then we name the ways it intersects with the analysis of self and society. At each step, reinterpretation is taking place. Each kind of critical reflection adds a layer of thought and pushes us, guided by the Holy Spirit, into deeper and more meaningful understandings. The starting point, however, is often the biblical text, with analysis of self and society added as a next-to-last step, before a final reinterpretation of the text.

In summary, the goal of critical-analytical reflection is to help adults listen deeply to both the text of the Bible and the text of their lives and describe meaningful understandings that arise when those two texts intersect. The critical-analytical color of Bible study allows a proper balance of subjectivity and objectivity, so that mind and heart are engaged and challenged.

Action: Ritual and Ministry

The adult learners have finished their long study of the David cycle. The teacher asks them to journal silently about what strikes them as the most important thing that they have learned. After a long period of silence, she invites them to create a prayer of thanksgiving out of their reflection: "We will begin each line with 'Thank you God for . . .' and each of you who wishes to will contribute the rest of the line." A group prayer is produced. The teacher then invites them to "brainstorm about what impact this story has on our faith and our society today. Does this call us to any action, ministry, or ways of thinking about the world?" After a lively discussion of this question, the study concludes with the prayer just created.

As I stated in the step "Responding" in chapter 3, we humans often find it easy to read and study, but more difficult to move into action. Furthermore, we often disagree about what actions we are called to take. Yet learning that does not result in change in behavior, as well as in feeling and thought, is not true learning. The third primary "color" of Bible study, therefore, must be action. Here we will explore different kinds of action that help Bible study engage our wills as well as our minds and hearts. One major kind of action consists of behavior on a personal and community level; in other words, it is the action of ministry. Another kind of action is formed by ritual and liturgy; these actions can provide faith foundations from which ministry is fed.

Action through Ritual and Liturgy

The main way in which biblical texts have been learned, assert some scholars, has been through ritual and prayer, "the liturgical reenactment and celebration of formative events."[36] Through the cycles of weeks and years, the celebration of special holy days, the stories "are remembered not just verbally but through the body."[37] Liturgical ritual is what makes stories into sacred texts.

Anthropologists have noted that those stories that give meaning and identity to a people are often learned, remembered, and celebrated through repetitive, formalized enactments called rituals.[38] Church scholars in our culture have picked up on these studies and have recognized how Christian liturgy, one kind of ritual, forms and shapes Christian community and its faith. Some scholars, however, have realized that not only can rituals create and establish, but new, alternative rituals can change older rituals, thereby bringing in new stories or new visions of old stories. These two different understandings can be called "traditional/authoritative rituals" and "emerging rituals."[39]

Traditional/Authoritative Rituals

Many of us carry strong memories of the worship services of our childhood, worship services filled with words, motions, silences, smells, visual symbols, and images that were woven together in a certain pattern of space and time. Our Christian liturgy is a specific kind of ritual, formed over the centuries within certain historical contexts. In ritual, the participants act. This action is formalized and set apart from ordinary space and time. Thus the participants are transported out of the ordinary, and the acts and symbols take on deep and meaningful implications. The very form of ritual teaches. Repetition (sometimes opposed with a one-time, unique act), rhythm, and order, whether of words, objects, or gestures, draw us in and add meaningful levels to images and actions.[40] In the Christian liturgical rites, therefore, we are not only worshiping God; we are enacting and embodying what we believe as a community of faith.

Ritual not only conserves culture by being traditional; it also conserves old traditions by adapting them within specific rites to the contemporary situation as, for example, changes in Roman Catholic and Episcopal liturgies.[41]

What can we learn from these studies about teaching the Bible? *A study of the Bible must include participation in the major forms of ritual of our tradition, namely the weekly worship service.*

Participation in the liturgies and rituals of the church is essential for several educational reasons. First, today's church member needs instruction to make explicit the connections between the symbols and stories of the biblical texts and the liturgy. Both the liturgy and the Bible study are made more meaningful by understanding how the biblical texts, symbols, and ideas are referred to and enacted in the worship service.

Second, Bible study cannot be divorced from weekly worship because such study must be rooted in the symbols, traditions, beliefs, and acts of a faithful community. Through such participation, in which the believer enacts the faith, the biblical stories become sacred texts. Such study without participation in the rites of the community could lead to sterile intellectualism or piously individualistic emotionalism.

Finally, and most importantly, we are called to participate in worship because we know that "the chief end of [humans] is to glorify God and enjoy [God] forever."[42] Traditionally, both the glorification and the enjoyment of God begin with the act of worship within the community of faith. In the worship service we open ourselves more fully to the guidance of the Holy Spirit, who is our guide to interpreting scripture and is found mostly strongly when "two or three are gathered" in the name of Jesus Christ.

Emerging Rituals

Ritual can also cause change, from simple kinds of adaptation to radical reorientation. Change through ritual happens, for example, when Jews and Christians, or other groups that normally do not meet, are asked to worship together.[43] Women have especially been in the forefront in creating new rituals in this society, in order to compensate for having been left out of formal, canonical ritual and stories for so long.[44] These rituals are often very meaningful to the women involved, whether they be a "croning ceremony" to celebrate a woman's fiftieth birthday or a healing service to mourn rape, incest, miscarriage, or abortion. Some take place within the boundaries of Christian tradition, simply reworking old elements of the liturgy. Others stand clearly outside the tradition. And some are on the boundaries, seen as a valid reworking of the tradition by some, and as scandalous, unorthodox, even heretical behavior by others.[45]

In conclusion, ritual is a kind of action that helps to teach the biblical texts. If the central teaching method of critical-analytical reflection is *dialogue*, and of disciplined imagination is *play*, the central teaching method in the dimension of ritual action is *performance*. Although the main goal of participants in ritual is to worship and celebrate God, the secondary outcome is learning. In traditional ritual, the adult student is rerooted in the symbols and beliefs of the community, allowing the interpretation of the Bible to take place in its proper context and keeping the study from abstract intellectualism or individualistic emotionalism. In emerging rituals, the work of God is celebrated in new interpretations and forms. The symbols and beliefs carried by the text are also carried by the enactment found in these rituals. Both of these kinds of ritual are valid and important forms of action and are essential to teaching and learning the Bible.

Through performance in the ritual we call worship, the stories, symbols, images, and ideas in the Bible are enacted and made real. This ritual performance is essential. This action makes of the Bible more than a collection of interesting stories or ancient history. The Bible becomes our story and our holy scripture.

In teaching, this color element can be applied in many ways. Rituals can emerge out of the group. Classes open and close with prayer. Different people are assigned to bring an opening litany or a meditative devotional. The sharing of "joys and concerns" can occur each week. All these acts are rituals, some within traditional forms, that develop within the classroom study setting. Teachers can encourage both traditional and emerging rituals in the following ways:

- Teachers can utilize what is already present, often informally, in the tradition: for example, opening and closing the session with prayer; linking prayer in with the biblical texts under study; asking others in the class to do so.
- Teachers can encourage use of biblical texts as the content of litanies, prayers, and benedictions: for example, by praying the psalms; using Paul's benedictions to close the session (the class could repeat the words aloud, for example); repeating biblical creeds, such as Deuteronomy 26:5–11, as affirmations of faith.
- Teachers can use the biblical texts in a ritual-like manner when it is appropriate: for example, following every reading with meditative silence; praying through a prayer in the text.
- The learning group can create responses to texts and to the sharing that the texts evoke: for example, creating new psalms or litanies of various sorts. These can continue traditional understandings, rewrite the text in a midrashic manner, or even wind up "talking against the text."[46] Ritual creation can also include dramatic responses such as skits, role-plays, mime, dance, hand movements, poems, and songs. As a teacher, I have introduced new songs about biblical persons. We have sung and danced to these songs. They have often become part of opening or closing rituals.[47]

Action through Ministry

In Ventura County, California, an American Baptist minister discovered that this agricultural community was destroying 50 percent of its food. Part of the problem was that the farmers plowed under whatever the picking machines missed after one pass through the fields. He and his congregation established a program in which teams (of mostly senior citizens) went into a field to glean after it was picked, with the farmer's permission. The newfound organization insured the gleaners so that the farmers would not worry about liability. The teams gleaned as much as they could carry in their trucks. The gleaners were allowed to keep some of the produce. The rest was stored locally and/or sent to the urban food banks of Los Angeles where it was distributed to the poor. Since the rich soil and mild climate of this area allows for three or four crops a year, the result was the redistribution of many fresh fruits and vegetables: lettuce, tomatoes, broccoli, cabbage, plums, oranges, and so on. One younger mother in my congregation in nearby Oxnard volunteered her truck and her time. She said to me, with deep joy, "I am helping others, and it is helping me. I feel like I am truly putting my faith into practice!"

This kind of action is often labeled "putting faith into practice." Although I dislike the dualism implicit in such a statement (opposing faith and practice), still it expresses what most of us think of when we think of action. It makes clear what this ingredient in teaching the Bible is about. The goal is obvious: we are to ask, "What does our encounter with the text call me and us to do?"

We can, however, move to the next question, "What am I to do?" too soon.[48] First, we must listen to and hear the text. Yet most of us Christians are already acting, hoping we are living out our faith. Therefore, not only after, but during the listening, we may find ourselves examining our actions in light of the new hearing. In doing so, we also reshape our vision of how we should and will act in the future.

Action of this kind, growing out of the question, "What does this encounter call me to do?" happens

on two interacting levels, personal and congregational. To become more faithful disciples of Christ
demands personal action: personal behaviors and
personal ministry. Faithfulness is also exercised by
the covenant community as a group, usually at the
congregational level. Furthermore, actions of ministry are required by individuals and congregations in
many different arenas, within the congregation and
outside the congregation in the arenas of community,
nation, and world. Actions of ministry can be interpersonal or social-political.

This educational element of action may seem
obvious, but it has traditionally been a difficult one
for us to master. We often leave our adult classes
without discussing either personal or political behavior. We are embarrassed to discuss personal issues,
and we are afraid of the pain of political controversy.
So we avoid both.

It takes a skillful teacher to help people reflect on
this kind of behavior and action. Many means can be
used to do this, means that will be determined by the
particular makeup of the group that one is teaching.
The following list is merely suggestive:

- The teacher may discuss with the group why behavior and action are so hard to talk about. The group
  may be able to devise strategies by which to talk
  about these issues and then to engage in action.
- Silent time may be set aside for journaling on personal
  behavior. These should not be shared or discussed.
- The group may covenant together to engage in some
  common form of ministry as a result of the study. It
  may decide on a period of time in which to come up
  with a plan (such as six weeks, or three months, or
  after a study of Luke).
- Bible study may be started with a group already in

active ministry, such as a group of gleaners, which can covenant to add a Bible study (the starting point of Bible study does not need to be the Bible).

- At the end of each class, participants may write down their decisions for personal and congregational action, and either keep them private, or share them, for example, in prayer.
- During discussions, teachers need to poke and prod with such thorny questions as "Does any of this have political implications?" or "What are the implications for enhancing justice in this society?" "What are *we* called to do together?" These can be discussed if trust has been built up. If not, discussion with a trusted partner or silent prayer might be appropriate.

In summary, the third primary color for the artist/teacher is action through ritual and ministry. The main educational method is performance, that is, doing what we feel God is calling us to do. This performance has a variety of forms: traditional and emerging rituals and personal and congregational ministry.

Conclusion

The artist/teacher now has on the palette the three basic elements that can be mixed to form a creative and sound Bible study. The mix will depend on the context, the teachers, and the learners. Just as some paintings use more yellow or more blue, so too the artist/teacher will find that different classes need more of one educational element than another, depending on their needs, learning styles, and experience with the Bible.

Artist/teachers will review regularly the study they are constructing to see if they are forgetting one of these colors and if it is needed. Creative teachers will also recognize that the ideas for using each of the colors described in this chapter are simply suggestive and will come up with other activities as well, depending in part on their own gifts. Teachers are invited to explore each of these colors, discover where their own gifts lie, and thereby experience the joy as well as the art of teaching.

Chapter Five

Ten Teaching Tips

The metaphor of the teacher as a painter has been used throughout this book in the hope that teachers will be inspired to work on their teaching methods and skills and then journey further, into the arena of inspired (in-Spirited) creativity, the area of art. The image of painter is only one artist image; other images could be more helpful to some teachers—images such as poet, musician, sculptor, potter, or weaver. In each one of these images, the artist must practice to become skilled in the methods appropriate to the medium. As those skills become honed, the artist begins to add that extra spark that makes the work art rather than simply a craft.

In this chapter I will speak directly to you, the artist/teacher, sharing with you teaching tips to guide you in your work as an artist/teacher. You may wish to adopt a different metaphor than that of the painter. As you will see, although the artist painter metaphor is useful, it also has limits (as is true of all metaphors used in this manner).

Tip 1: Remember Your Mission as a Teacher, to the Adult Students and to the Bible.

"Why do you teach the Bible study in your church?" the denominational executive asked the assembled Bible study

leaders. The answers were varied, but a common theme was that of helping people see that they needed to change their beliefs, their behavior, or their lifestyles.

Too often, teachers believe that their job is to change the people they are teaching. Teachers who favor the educational goal of *conversion* or the educational goal of *justice and faith in action* (see chapter 1) carry this concern most strongly. In a way they are operating out of the artist metaphor, envisioning the learners as the blank canvas that needs paint.

Yet this is the point at which our metaphor of painting can be interpreted erroneously—for both educational and theological reasons. Educationally, as we have seen in our discussion of adult learners in chapter 2, adults are not canvases on which teachers paint. Adults are actors in their own learning, not passive recipients of someone else's knowledge. Therefore they must be treated as active investigators and as co-learners with the teacher. They become teachers to each other and to themselves. We teachers are to guide this explorative learning process and to learn along with them.[1]

We must treat our adult students as active explorers and co-learners for theological reasons as well. Every human being is a child of God, valued by God, and therefore not an object to be manipulated or reshaped. Jesus equated even "the least" as representing himself (Matt. 25:40). So too every adult is to be treated with the care we would give our Lord. It is God's task, not ours, to change and convert through the working of the Holy Spirit in each heart. We teachers can be the Spirit's helpers in many ways, but only when we understand our role and mission.

Our mission to the students is to open up the Bible

and make it accessible by providing an educational process that is helpful to adult learners.[2] Using our palette of primary colors we fashion a teaching process that helps to illuminate the Bible and contemporary life. The teachers and learners together paint their interpretation of God's Word for their lives. Their picture illustrates what the biblical texts they are studying mean for them. By utilizing a wide variety of teaching methods and tools, we provide more possibilities for our learners, with their different learning styles and gifts, to create their own pictures of what the Bible means for them.

Our mission to the Bible as the Word of God is to listen to its texts carefully, to present many ways by which it can be heard and interpreted, and to be guided by the Holy Spirit. The five Rs model in chapter 3, or the three primary colors of chapter 4, present methods to listen with our hearts and minds to the texts, to listen both more objectively and more subjectively, and to respond with our actions so that we can live faithfully as God's children and Christ's disciples.

Tip 2: Know and Respect Your Adult Students.

The new Christian education director visited the two Bible study groups in her church: one group met Sunday morning; the other was a weekday women's Bible study. She was struck by the different styles of teaching and learning present in each group. The Sunday morning group listened to lectures or watched videos about the biblical text, with a little discussion afterwards and almost no personal storytelling. The weekday group shared stories, including many personal ones, and seemed to jump in and out of study of the actual text.

Groups and individuals take on particular styles of learning that they prefer. In the above scenario, the educational styles have become set, and much is being omitted as a result: the Sunday group may not be linking the study to their own stories; and the weekday group may be lacking a deeper listening to the text. Both these groups need to experience new ways of learning. Yet before initiating any change in their educational routines, the teacher needs to know more about the learners: Is this the style most of the class prefers, or is this style an easy and old habit? Are there teaching elements that could be introduced that fit in with the style already in place but that would increase the connections between biblical texts and contemporary lives?

Knowing and respecting our students takes time, patience, an observant eye, and a listening ear. Which adults never ask questions or talk? Why is that? Which ones seem especially appreciative of the story videotapes or the biblical atlases? We teachers can enlist the students' help by asking them to name and evaluate the ways in which they learn best.

Respecting our learners also means treating what they already know and are willing to share with care and respect. When we disagree, we can be honest about our disagreements and still work with them as partners searching out the meaning of the biblical passage. It can be helpful to identify the various understandings of the Bible that may be causing major differences in interpretation, as described in chapter 1. Balancing these different, even sometimes opposite, interpretations with respect does take practice and is indeed an art.

Tip 3: Plan and Prepare
with a Partner if Possible.

Nancy and Lori were each excellent teachers of different classes. Each one was prepared and creative, loving her students and her teaching. One summer they were asked to teach a Vacation Bible Study class together. The results were impressive and exciting. By working together, they said, they were forced to prepare even more carefully. Best of all, they sparked ideas in each other that they would not have come up with by themselves.

As experienced teachers know, the class process teaches as much as the content. In fact the process *is* content. Just as the artist plans his painting before applying the paint, the artist/teacher pays great attention to planning an effective educational process guided by models such as the five Rs. Effective planning must be done sufficiently in advance in order to review the overall goals, to determine the current objectives, to decide on educational activities, and to locate the necessary resources. Planning includes remembering each student and his or her individual needs and learning styles. It also includes evaluating how past lessons worked and mulling over ways they could have been improved. All this takes some time.

I confess that too many times I have left my planning to the last minute and then could not locate the video, cassette tape, piece of art, or concordance that would have made the lesson far more interesting and educational. Last-minute planning has also meant that I tended to fall into using one kind of teaching method far more often than another. Yet planning ahead can be satisfying and fun, a chance to think creatively about the next lessons, to pray for oneself and the students, and to engage in a treasure hunt for good resources.

Planning with a partner teacher is especially effective. In my experience, the ideas that grow out of two minds are more than the sum of their separate thoughts. Something new happens when two teachers enjoy working together; creative sparks fly, interesting activities are invented, and new resources are discovered or made. A teaching partner also helps us become more aware of our own assumptions and interpretations (see chapter 1). Two teachers in a class allow for more teaching-learning styles to be used and for more careful observation and knowledge of the students and their needs. Of course, teachers do not always work well together, and such pairing needs to be done carefully.

Tip 4: Pay Attention to the Class Environment.

I was invited to teach the adult Bible class in a small Texas town. The class was held, I discovered, in the fellowship hall. During the hour that I was there, I observed a stream of children and adults walking through in order to use the one bathroom. Others showed up to make the coffee in the corner kitchen. The blackboard behind me was so old and covered with yellow chalk dust that I had to abandon the idea of writing on it. While the adults were appreciative of the class and seemed oblivious to the activities around them, some did complain at times that they were having a hard time hearing me and each other.

When we are very familiar with our surroundings, we often fail to notice them. The stranger invited to teach, however, will notice that there is an old, unused blackboard in the corner or that the noisy coffeepot makes hearing difficult in the echoing fellowship hall. As we saw in chapter 2, environment is important for adults as well as children. We will work hard to brighten up children's rooms and make the environment pleasant and educational; but we fail to do so for adults for whom hearing, seeing, and sitting may be something of a challenge. A pleasing environment is also encouraging for the teacher. Just as the artist needs a lot of daylight and a certain kind of space with good tools, so too the artist/teacher needs a quiet area with light, good sound transmission, and working tools such as black or white boards.

Changing the environment is an opportunity to teach. The teacher can decorate the room with pictures illustrating the biblical texts or art created by the adults as part of the "disciplined imagination" activities. Adult learners can often be invited to participate in setting up the space in ways that are helpful and pleasing for learning.

Tip 5: Build in Layers of Reflection on the Biblical Texts.

In a study of healing stories, the class began with Mark 2:1–12. The teacher asked one person to read the story out loud as the rest of the group followed in their Bibles. He then invited them to close their eyes and led them in a meditation in which they were guided through the story imagining themselves to be the paralytic carried by friends to the feet of Jesus. The class closed with silent reflection and journaling on their experience. In the next session, the class returned to the text, looking at its context in Mark and asking historical questions. Later the class discussed healing in our society and their community, especially in reference to this text. The participants returned to the text and wrote a prayer of healing to be used in worship the fol-lowing Sunday.

Returning to a biblical passage again and again has proven to be very effective in my and other pastors' experiences of teaching Bible study (see chapters 2 and 3). Each visit to the text allows for new questions to be asked and for additional insights. Each visit to the text can employ different educational processes: oral and silent readings, dramatizations, guided med-itations, historical analysis, midrashic retellings, poem and prayer creations, music, and movement. These layers of reflection on the text function in sev-eral ways: they allow different learners to experience their favorite modes of learning; they teach a variety of tools with which to study the Bible; they open up the biblical passages in more depth; and they allow more ways in which the text of our lives can connect with the biblical texts.

Tip 6: Make Silence a Helpful Tool.

After the prayer of confession in Sunday morning wor-ship, the pastor built in a "moment of silent confession." After thirty seconds, according to her watch, feet started to shuffle, and by sixty seconds, coughs and whispers could be heard as people wondered what they were supposed to do.

We teachers are often intimidated when we set out a discussion question and no one begins to talk. "I can't get my adults to have a discussion," many teach-ers lament. As the above example shows, our society values talking and sharing more than silence. A lack of response can indeed be a problem. Yet silence is as necessary an educational ingredient in teaching adults as rests are in musical compositions. Silence allows the adult learner to reflect, think, feel, react, and move on to new ideas, thoughts, and feelings.

Silence can be built in by the teacher in a variety of ways. It is the central ingredient of prayer. It takes the form of journaling, jotting notes and ideas, quiet or guided meditations, and writing poems and psalms. Silence becomes the rests between the layers of reflection. It can give additional shape to the central educational activities.

Silence can also be the awkward pause after a question has been raised; such silence can be accepted and allowed to continue for a while. If after a long silence no one is willing to answer, the question may need to be reworded or dropped. The adults can evaluate why they were unable or unwilling to discuss at that point.

Silent meditation is an ancient tool of prayer in the Christian tradition. In today's world this technique of prayer is both a luxury and a necessity. The teacher who makes silence her friend gives a gift to the students.

Tip 7: Be Flexible within Limits.

Most of us have experienced the inflexible teacher. The lesson has to be finished, no matter what. The interesting issue just raised by a student, which may send us down a different road for awhile, is ignored and negatively criticized. We have left the class frustrated and dissatisfied. We have also experienced the overly flexible teacher who allowed every tangent to be discussed and, as a result, never brought the class back to the stated goal of the study. We left the class frustrated and dissatisfied.

Appropriate flexibility is part of the art of good teaching. Flexibility in relation to the students allows for their interests and needs to connect with the subject being studied. The tangents raised by questions and stories that are shared may be more important and interesting than the material we teachers have prepared. They may help make the connection between the biblical passages and the lives of the learners.

Some groups, however, have participants who constantly derail the discussion with their personal story and or tangential ideas. Class members often will express their frustration to the teacher about this. When these occurrences become too frequent, we teachers need to take charge and firmly bring the discussion back to the study at hand. Sometimes we have to talk with the person after the class and ask for fewer interruptions. This guidance, in and out of class, can be done with gentle firmness. We are aware that we may alienate and lose that member of the class, but we accept that risk for the good of the larger group.

Flexibility is also necessary when following a curricular model, such as the five Rs in chapter 3, or when putting together a plan based on the educational dimensions in chapter 4. I find it helpful to plan for more educational activities than necessary, in case some prove not to be productive. Curricular flexibility means quickly dropping a teaching activity when it becomes evident that it is not interesting or is leading to misunderstanding. The artist/teacher creates his art in response to the students and their interaction with the biblical text. He will note how the students respond and will shift when necessary. This flexibility, however, still keeps to the goals and objectives and continues to involve all three "colors" of Bible study at various times.

Tip 8: Offer Adults Some Control
Over Their Learning.

Sometimes when I have closed a class with the singing and dancing of the song "We are dancing Sarah's circle" (sung to the tune of "We are climbing Jacob's ladder"), some participants have told me that they normally do not like to do "this kind of thing." Since the rest of the class consisted of more analytical activities, however, they "put up with it." I thanked them and remembered to go easy on creative movement with that group.

Adults have spent a lot of time learning how to be in charge of their lives. As we have discussed in chapter 2, they do not like to be treated as children or to lose control. As learners, they appreciate being given choices, being encouraged to voice their opinions, and having their evaluations taken seriously. Giving adults some control does not necessarily mean having them list what they want to study, although it can include this possibility. Many adults, however, do not want to have to figure out what they need to learn. They prefer instead to be offered a choice of classes, of teachers, or of types of classes. Some prefer large lecture classes, for example, while others like small intimate studies. Some wish to be offered the option of study of societal issues that are related back to the Bible, while others would choose a Bible study of a book like the Gospel of Luke. Adults may exert some control by giving feedback to the teacher about how much they like or dislike a certain kind of activity. They expect a serious reply showing that the comment was taken seriously.

Artist/teachers need to look for ways to give adult learners some control in their own learning. Treating adults as co-learners and taking them and their different styles seriously helps this to happen.

Tips 9 and 10: Pray. Be Open to the Holy Spirit.

In my work with Christian education programs in churches, the wish I have heard most often from teachers has been that they could regularly gather together for prayer. In churches where teachers were able to meet weekly or monthly for prayer, the teachers stated it helped them feel happier in their teaching, more able to love their students, and more likely to be open to God's guidance.

In our praying we invoke the Holy Spirit to guide us as we interpret the scriptures for our lives in today's world, asking that, as the Spirit guided the writers of the biblical texts, it may guide us, the readers of the texts. We pray for ourselves as teachers who are also learning and for our adult learners, that through our study we may all become more faithful disciples of Jesus Christ. Prayer can open us to seeing each person more in the way God sees each person and make us more effective and loving teachers. Our prayer allows us to leave the work of conversion and change to God through the Holy Spirit.

To be inspired means to be in-Spirited with the Holy Spirit. The creative moment of teaching, the unexpected "aha!" the surprising personal story—all these and more can happen when artist/teachers allow their knowledge and skills to be open to the guidance of the Holy Spirit. To be engaged in the art of teaching is to be continually aware of the presence of God in the classroom.

Teaching can be frustrating and difficult. It can be

interesting and fun. Teaching always involves challenges. With experience and practice, it does become easier and can evolve into an artistic process. With God the great Artist/Teacher as a guide, we are given the joyous gift of joining with God in teaching God's children called "adults."

Notes

Introduction

1. This expression dating from the Reformation can be found in the Westminster Confession of 1647 and is discussed in *Presbyterian Understanding and Use of Holy Scripture*, a position statement adopted by the 123d General Assembly (1983) of the Presbyterian Church (U.S.A.) (Louisville, Ky.: Office of the General Assembly, Presbyterian Church (U.S.A.), 1992), 1–6.

Chapter 1: Educational Goals and Biblical Interpretation

1. For a discussion of the way in which key biblical images and metaphors shape interpretation, see Sallie McFague, *Metaphorical Theology* (Philadelphia: Fortress, 1982), 23–29.
2. Dorothy Jean Furnish, *Exploring the Bible with Children* (Nashville: Abingdon, 1975), 29–30.
3. Ibid. 31–50. See also, for example, Thomas H. Groome, *Christian Religious Education: Sharing Our Story and Vision* (San Francisco: Harper & Row, 1980).
4. James D. Smart, *The Strange Silence of the Bible in the Church: A Study in Hermeneutics* (Philadelphia: Westminster, 1970), 136.
5. Ibid., 144.
6. Iris V. Cully, *Imparting the Word: The Bible in Christian Education* (Philadelphia: Westminster, 1962), 16.
7. See Karl Barth, *Dogmatics in Outline* (New York, Harper & Row, 1959), for a good summary of this affirmation.
8. Smart, *The Strange Silence of the Bible in the Church*, 116.
9. Ibid., especially 141–63.
10. James A. Sanders, *From Sacred Story to Sacred Text* (Philadelphia: Fortress, 1987), 17.

125

11. Ibid., 163–72.
12. Ibid., 65.
13. Ibid., 52, 57.
14. Ibid., 163–72. See also Sanders, *Canon and Community: A Guide to Canonical Criticism* (Philadelphia: Fortress, 1984), 50–60, for a discussion of five major biblical hermeneutics.
15. The best-known educator who favors this model is Thomas H. Groome, *Christian Religious Education*.
16. George Albert Coe, *A Social Theory of Religious Education* (New York: Charles Scribner's Sons, 1924), 68. This discussion of Coe is drawn from this work and also from his *Education in Religion and Morals* (Chicago: Revell, 1904).
17. Unlike Coe, who had an optimistic, hopeful view of his American society of that time, today's liberation theologians are critical of contemporary society and of interpretations of the Bible that sustain the status quo. For both, however, the goal is similar: to bring about profound societal transformation for justice through the reappropriation of biblical symbols and principles.
18. See for example, Letty Russell, *Growth in Partnership* (Philadelphia: Westminster, 1981), 63ff., and *Household of Freedom* (Philadelphia: Westminster, 1987), 27–28. The Exodus story is also used as paradigmatic by Latin American liberation theologians such as Gustavo Gutiérrez, *A Theology of Liberation* (Maryknoll, NY: Orbis, 1973).
19. Russell replaces the image of "kingdom" with "household of freedom."
20. For feminist and womanist theologians, some texts themselves can also be viewed with suspicion, as attempts to keep women in inferior, less powerful roles than men. For more on this problem, see, for example, Elisabeth Schüssler Fiorenza's introduction in *Bread Not Stone* (Boston: Beacon, 1984) and John A. Phillips, *Eve—the History of an Idea* (San Francisco: Harper & Row, 1984).
21. For most people, the purpose of reading the Bible is for personal transformation, asserts Walter Wink, *The Bible in Human Transformation* (Philadelphia: Fortress, 1973), 2.
22. Cully, *Imparting the Word*, 16.
23. Ibid., 20–24, 47–56.
24. Iris V. Cully, *Education for Spiritual Growth* (San Francisco: Harper & Row, 1984), 121–22.
25. We remember, for example, Catherine of Siena in the fourteenth century, who took care of those stricken by the plague,

worked for peace between Siena and Florence, taught a circle of disciples, and chastised the pope for the decadence of his court and for continuing to live in Avignon instead of Rome. See Catherine of Siena, *The Dialogue* (New York: Paulist Press, 1980).

26. At the time of this writing, for example, spirituality courses and continuing education programs are being offered in the majority of Presbyterian Church (U.S.A.) seminaries. Many of these started in the late 1990s.

27. Walter Brueggemann also demonstrates the way different biblical texts educate in different ways. The Torah story, he declares, establishes our identity. It tells us who we are. The writings of the prophets disrupt our comfortable view of reality in order to help us identify injustice. These texts call us to work for the widow and the orphan, to establish justice and shalom. Finally, the wisdom writings impart some human wisdom for everyday life, a life obedient to God. They help us understand both the glory of human knowledge and its limitations. They open up for us the limitless mystery of God (*The Creative Word: Canon as a Model of Biblical Education* [Philadelphia: Fortress, 1982]; see also his book *The Prophetic Imagination* [Philadelphia: Fortress, 1978]).

Chapter 2: Adults Learn Best When . . .

1. Sharan B. Merriam and Rosemary S. Caffarella, *Learning in Adulthood: A Comprehensive Guide* (San Francisco: Jossey-Bass, 1991), 86.

2. Mezirow defines learning as "the process of making a new or revised interpretation of the meaning of an experience, which guides subsequent understanding, appreciation, and action." He identifies two kinds of learning, instrumental and communicative. Instrumental learning is learning how to do something. Communicative learning is learning that seeks to "understand what is meant by another through speech, writing, drama, art, or dance" (Jack Mezirow and Associates, *Fostering Critical Reflection in Adulthood: A Guide to Transformative and Emancipatory Learning* [San Francisco: Jossey-Bass, 1990], 1).

3. When we speak of learning in this chapter, we will not be distinguishing among different types of learning. The picture painted of "how adults learn best" applies in general throughout the learning spiral. However, the differences in learning

noted above are visible in some parts of the picture, namely in the area of critical reflection.

4. A modified version of this chapter first appeared in my article "Understanding Adult Learners: Challenges for Theological Education," *Theological Education* 34, no. 1 (Autumn 1997): 11–24.

5. Mark Tennant, "The Psychology of Adult Teaching and Learning," in John M. Peters, Peter Jarvis and Associates, *Adult Education: Evolution and Achievements in a Developing Field of Study* (San Francisco: Jossey-Bass, 1991), 198.

6. John M. Hull, *What Prevents Christian Adults from Learning?* (Philadelphia: Trinity Press International, 1991), chapter 1.

7. Alan B. Knox, *Adult Development and Learning* (San Francisco: Jossey-Bass, 1989), 456.

8. Paulo Freire, *Pedagogy of the Oppressed* (New York: Seabury, 1973), 77–79.

9. Leon McKenzie, *The Religious Education of Adults* (Birmingham, Ala.: Religious Education Press, 1982), 95, 101.

10. Studies of motivation in learning often focus on self-esteem, ideal self, and expectations. See Tennant, "The Psychology of Adult Teaching and Learning," 204–6.

11. Ibid., 209.

12. Ibid.

13. Robert Redfield defines worldview as a broad category that covers patterns of thought, comprehensive attitudes toward life, and conceptions of what ought to be and what is. Worldview is especially important because of "the suggestion it carries of the structure of things as man is aware of them. It is . . . the way we see ourselves in relation to all else" (*The Primitive World and Its Transformations* [Ithaca: Cornell University Press, 1953], 86).

14. See the study documents *Presbyterian Understanding and Use of Holy Scripture* and *Biblical Authority and Interpretation* (Louisville, Ky.: Office of the General Assembly, Presbyterian Church [U.S.A.], 1992).

15. C. Ellis Nelson, *How Faith Matures* (Louisville, Ky.: Westminster/John Knox Press, 1989), especially 151 ff.

16. Cyril O. Houle, *The Literature of Adult Education: A Bibliographic Essay* (San Francisco: Jossey-Bass, 1992), 291. This phenomenon is very apparent in Doctor of Ministry programs in theological institutions. When persons with experience in

an area join together to engage in new learning and are open to learning from each other, exciting education occurs.

17. For example, Malcolm Knowles, *The Adult Learner*, 3d ed. (Houston: Gulf Publishing Co., 1984), 189–91, 219.

18. Freire, *Pedagogy of the Oppressed*, especially 75–85.

19. Knowles states, "None but the humble become good teachers of adults. In an adult class the student's experience counts for as much as the teacher's knowledge" (*The Adult Learner*, 98).

20. Helpful studies of the importance of mentoring include Laurent A. Daloz, *Effective Teaching and Mentoring* (San Francisco: Jossey-Bass, 1986); Sondra Higgins Matthaei, *FaithMatters: Faith-Mentoring in the Faith Community* (Valley Forge, Pa.: Trinity Press International, 1996); *Effective Christian Education: A National Study of Protestant Congregations* (Minneapolis: Search Institute, 1990). See too Houle, *The Literature of Adult Education*, 302–3.

21. Matthaei also names four kinds of mentoring: guide, model, guarantor, mediator (*Faith Matters*, 50–77).

22. Dennis Patience, "Listening to the People: A Prerequisite for Planning Adult Education Events" (Doctor of Ministry project: Austin Presbyterian Theological Seminary, 1998).

23. See Daloz, *Effective Teaching and Mentoring*, xvii.

24. See Knowles, *The Adult Learner*; Merriam and Caffarella, *Learning in Adulthood*, 28–32; McKenzie, *The Religious Education of Adults*.

25. Knowles, *The Adult Learner*, 118.

26. Merriam and Caffarella (*Learning in Adulthood*, 87) cite studies by Houle and others.

27. Knowles, *The Adult Learner*, 121.

28. This belief has been unintentionally reinforced by cognitive development theories, such as that of Jean Piaget. Piaget studied the way children understood concepts differently in different stages of development. The adult way of grasping concepts he named "formal operations." This stage of thinking enables the adult to think symbolically and abstractly, without the need for concrete props or examples. Formal operations thinking, reached usually in young adulthood, seems to represent the last step in mature cognitive development.

More recently, however, researchers have engaged in more careful studies of the adult throughout life. These studies suggest that there are many ways of thinking and knowing in adulthood. See, for example, Belenky, Clinchy, Goldberger and Tarule's studies of different ways of knowing in adult women (*Women's Ways of Knowing* [New York: Basic, 1986]). Boucouvalas and Krupp cite several different ways researchers have looked at adult cognition; they suggest that these studies of adults indicate the need to "cultivate" a variety of ways of knowing—cognitive, contemplative, and dialectical (Marcie Boucouvalas with Judy-Arin Krupp, "Adult Development and Learning," in *Handbook of Adult and Continuing Education*, ed. Sharan B. Merriam and Phyllis M. Cunningham [San Francisco: Jossey-Bass, 1990]). Some have added a fifth stage to Piaget's four stages: after formal operations is the stage of "postformal thinking." This stage includes moving to relativistic thinking and then to dialectical thinking "whereby one is able to reconcile previously considered antithetical thought into a greater whole." Other studies suggest six stages of structures of consciousness found in those who practiced meditation and nine stages of adult knowing. The last three of these adult stages deal with inner insight and personal development through an integration of thought and experience.

29. This discussion is drawn from Knox, *Adult Development and Learning*, 409ff., and Tennant, "The Psychology of Adult Teaching and Learning," 199–202.

30. Tennant, "The Psychology of Adult Teaching and Learning," 199.

31. Knox, *Adult Development and Learning*, 421.

32. Developmental psychologists such as Erik Erikson, Jean Piaget, and Lawrence Kohlberg all point to cognitive dissonance as the source of discomfort that pushes individuals to new developmental tasks and ways of thinking. See also Tennant, *Adult Development and Learning*, 207.

33. Stephen D. Brookfield, "Facilitating Adult Learning," in *Handbook of Adult and Continuing Education*, ed. Merriam and Cunningham, 206.

34. Hull, *What Prevents Christian Adults from Learning?* 98–99.

35. Knox, *Adult Development and Learning*, 433. Knox finds that the choice to accept the challenge or to withdraw from learning seems to be a function of personality, experience, and situation, rather than of age.

36. Ibid., 96–111.

37. In my experience, the term "reflection" is often misunderstood or subject to a variation of definitions. Beginners in doctoral programs who are asked to engage in "theological reflection" often produce discourses on what they like or dislike about certain theological ideas. Some seminary professors have also shared with me that for them the term "reflection" implies sitting back and sharing feelings. While reflecting on feelings is important, educators mean more than that when they utilize this term. It must also include elements of analysis and evaluation. Of course, the emotional and intellectual cannot truly be separated. True knowing involves both capacities in one inseparable broth.

38. Walter Ellis, paper for a Doctor of Ministry course, 1991. The author created his questions based on the model of theological reflection presented by James and Evelyn Eaton Whitehead, *Method in Ministry* (New York: Seabury, 1980).

39. In another project, the pastor was investigating how a certain lay ministry training program with ten training sessions affected the participants' understanding of ministry. She was interested, not in what they had learned, but in how what they had learned affected them and had changed their ideas and beliefs. While all the participants filled out questionnaires at the end of the whole course, a small group of five was picked to be interviewed a day or two after each training session. The five interviewed reported at the end of the program that they had learned so much more from the training because they knew that they would be questioned about the meaning of each session. They were therefore more conscious of what they were learning during the training sessions and how it affected them. They also took time to think back on each training session after it was over in anticipation of the interview. The interview then required them to articulate some of the reflection they had undertaken. The result was a deeper, certainly more self-conscious, learning than that of the other participants (Donna Knight, paper for a Doctor of Ministry course at Austin Presbyterian Theological Seminary, 1991).

40. I would urge educators not to jump too quickly to judgment about whether reflection engaged in by a group is critical reflection or not. What is critical reflection for some may not be for others. The act of truly transformative thinking is made possible by the Holy Spirit. The educator sets up the

possibilities for it to happen. In addition, although I believe critical reflection to be extremely important, not all learning can bring paradigm shifts. Much learning is quantitative, deepening, and expanding.

41. Knox, *Adult Development and Learning*, 442–43.

42. Knowles, *The Adult Learner*, 58.

43. Knox, *Adult Development and Learning*, 439.

44. Knowles, *The Adult Learner*, 59–60.

45. McKenzie, *The Religious Education of Adults*, 95.

46. See Knowles, *The Adult Learner*, 57, and Tennant, "The Psychology of Adult Teaching," 197–99.

47. Knowles, *The Adult Learner*, 61.

48. Knox states that "effective adult learning typically entails an active search for meaning and discovery of relationships between current competence and new learning" (*Adult Development and Learning*, 433). Sharon Parks bases much of her work on the need of young adults to make meaning in their lives. Erikson's categories of generativity and integrity include a deepening of meaning for one's work and for one's existence.

49. Brookfield, "Facilitating Adult Learning," 204–5.

50. See Knox, *Adult Development and Learning*, 451–55; and Boucouvalas with Krupp, "Adult Development and Learning," 191.

51. Knowles, *The Adult Learner*, 119.

52. Knox, *Adult Development and Learning*, 468.

53. See the works of Howard Gardner, especially. A good summary is found in his *Multiple Intelligences: The Theory in Practice* (New York: Basic Books, 1993).

54. Knowles, *The Adult Learner*, 137. I have also found contracts to be useful with both parents and youth in youth confirmation classes.

55. Knox, *Adult Development and Learning*, 455.

56. McKenzie, "The Religious Education of Adults," 128–33.

57. Knox states that "when prior learning is similar but different in some important respects, it often interferes with the new learning" (*Adult Development and Learning*, 439).

58. Walter Brueggemann, *The Creative Word: Canon as a Model for Biblical Education* (Philadelphia: Fortress, 1982), 14–17.

59. For a discussion of the way imagination leads to models in science, see Sallie McFague, *Metaphorical Theology* (Philadelphia: Fortress, 1982), chapter 3.

60. Dennis Patience gives this example in his doctoral project, "Listening to the People," and concludes that teaching may begin with action as well as result in action.

61. Judith Plaskow, "Jewish Memory from a Feminist Perspective," in *Weaving the Visions: New Patterns in Feminist Spirituality*, ed. Judith Plaskow and Carol P. Christ (San Francisco: Harper & Row, 1989), 48. Anthropologists recognize that rituals keep the meaning of symbols and stories alive and relevant.

Chapter 3: The Five Rs Model of Bible Study

1. It is remarkable, for example, how many products use the name or story of Eve for marketing purposes (I have seen Eve referenced to sell automobiles, underwear, lotions, and feminine hygiene products).

2. In fact, the idea for this step came, in part, from Elisabeth Schüssler Fiorenza's "hermeneutics of remembrance," discussed in her *Bread Not Stone* (Boston: Beacon, 1984), and was affirmed by a step in John Alsup's method of biblical exegesis ("The Role of Listening in Biblical Interpretation," *Austin Seminary Bulletin: Faculty Edition* 92, no. 8 [May 1977]: 7–25).

3. We do not ever remove human experience from interpretation in order to hear an "original meaning" that is God's true Word for all time. Human experience matures, however, and adults can learn to hear the text in new ways, as God's Spirit guides them.

4. See Raymond E. Brown, *The Community of the Beloved Disciple* (New York: Paulist, 1979).

5. The discussion of principles of biblical interpretation is taken from my study of the pastoral epistles (Christine E. Blair, "The Pastoral Epistles," in the *Adult Foundational Curriculum, The Bible Speaks*, Unit 1, 1997–98) and is strongly informed by *Presbyterian Understanding and Use of Holy Scripture/Biblical Authority and Interpretation* (Louisville, Ky.: Office of the General Assembly, Presbyterian Church (U.S.A.), 1992).

6. John H. Hayes and Carl R. Holladay, *Biblical Exegesis: A Beginner's Handbook*, rev. ed. (Atlanta: John Knox Press, 1987), 45.

7. See Robert Alter, *The Art of Biblical Narrative* (New York: Basic Books, 1981), 178–86.

8. See chapter 4 on education based in story; in this step, critical analysis and story interweave.

9. Blair, "The Pastoral Epistles," 4–6.

10. Declaration by the Southern Baptist Convention, June 2000. See PCUSA "News Briefs," note #5939, 16 June 2000.
11. See Blair, "The Pastoral Epistles."
12. These examples come from my experience as a pastor and from the ministries of my Doctor of Ministry pastors.
13. Judith Plaskow, "Jewish Memory from a Feminist Perspective," in *Weaving the Visions: New Patterns in Feminist Spirituality*, ed. Judith Plaskow and Carol P. Christ (San Francisco: Harper & Row, 1989), 47.

Chapter 4: The Three Primary Colors of Bible Study

1. There are some similarities between my three educational "colors" and the "sides of the faith cube" developed by Richard Robert Osmer in *Teaching for Faith* (Louisville, Ky.: Westminster/John Knox Press, 1992), although we worked independently.
2. James Fowler, *Stages of Faith* (San Francisco: Harper & Row, 1981). Fowler's understanding of faith as imagination serves as a foundation for our discussion. He states: "Faith as an imaginative process is awakened and shaped . . . by the images, symbols, rituals and conceptual representations, offered with conviction, in the language and common life of those with whom we learn and grow" (25). Faith, then, is an active mode of knowing, of composing a felt sense or image of the condition of our lives taken as a whole. Faith is "an alignment of the will, a resting of the heart, in accordance with a vision of transcendent value and power, one's ultimate concern" (14).
3. From William R. White, *Stories for the Journey* (Minneapolis: Augsburg, 1988), 102–3.
4. Katherine Pfisterer Darr, *Far More Precious than Jewels: Perspectives on Biblical Women* (Louisville, Ky.: Westminster/John Knox Press, 1991), 29–34.
5. For a more thorough discussion of midrash, see Jacob Neusner, *What Is Midrash?* (Philadelphia: Fortress, 1987) and his *Midrash in Context: Exegesis in Formative Judaism* (Philadelphia: Fortress, 1983).
6. Judith Plaskow, "Jewish Memory from a Feminist Perspective," in *Weaving the Visions: New Patterns in Feminist Spirituality*, ed. Judith Plaskow and Carol P. Christ (San Francisco: Harper & Row, 1989), 46.
7. Ibid.

8. Robert L. Short, *The Gospel according to Peanuts* (Richmond: John Knox Press, 1965), 32.

9. From Josepha Sherman, *Rachel the Clever and Other Jewish Folktales* (Little Rock, Ark.: August House Publishers, 1993), 53–55.

10. Short, *The Gospel according to Peanuts*, 26.

11. The kernel of this idea is from William J. Bausch, *Storytelling: Imagination and Faith* (Mystic, Conn.: Twenty-Third Publications, 1964), 15–16.

12. Ibid., 171.

13. Short affirms that "art is one of the most eloquent and influential voices of any culture. It not only expresses the hopes, fears, and needs of a culture, but it also provides its own unique vocabulary of signs and symbols in which these needs are expressed" (*The Gospel according to Peanuts*, 13).

14. Bausch, *Storytelling*, 27.

15. White, *Stories for the Journey*, 11.

16. Bausch, *Storytelling*, 171, 58, 60.

17. The works of Carl Jung, Mircea Eliade, and Joseph Campbell speak to this issue of symbols and archetypes.

18. C. S. Lewis, *The Lion, the Witch, and the Wardrobe* (London: Collins, 1974), 168.

19. Martha Ann Kirk, *God of Our Mothers* (Albany, Calif.: Loretto Spirituality Network); this resource consists of two cassette tapes with the stories of seven biblical women.

20. Ursula K. LeGuin, "She Unnames Them," in *Buffalo Gals and Other Animal Presences* (New York: NAL Penguin, 1987), 194–96.

21. I owe this idea to Dr. Karen Jo Torjesen and a retreat she led many years ago in southern California.

22. See my articles "Dramatization," "Pageantry," and "Roleplaying" in *Encyclopedia of Religious Education*, ed. Iris and Kendig Cully (San Francisco: Harper & Row, 1990).

23. Adults, like children, can be given a structure for writing poems: the haiku, for example, is seventeen syllables over three lines (first and third lines with five syllables, seven on the second) and invokes images, especially of the seasons; many children's curricula give structures for cinquains, for psalms, and for other poetic forms. I often teach the group to write a group poem or prayer together, beginning each line with an agreed upon phrase, such as "Thank you, God, for . . ." "We praise you for . . ." "We weep for . . ." "We long for . . ."

24. This phrase was coined by Nelle Morton, *The Journey Is Home* (Boston: Beacon, 1985), 18.

25. Thomas H. Groome, *Christian Religious Education* (San Francisco: Harper & Row, 1980). Groome's method is one very effective way to weave storytelling throughout the religious education process; his thoughts have been very helpful to me. See especially chapters 9 and 10.

26. John H. Hayes and Carl R. Hollady, *Biblical Exegesis: A Beginner's Handbook*, rev. ed. (Atlanta: John Knox Press, 1987), 26.

27. Of course, historical-critical analysis is not empty of personal feeling and bias. The very questions we ask and the manner in which we approach the texts presuppose some interpretation and assumptions on our part. For a good history of this idea, see Groome's discussion in *Christian Religious Education*, 152–83.

28. James Michael Lee, *The Content of Religious Instruction* (Birmingham, Ala.: Religious Education Press, 1985), 177–83.

29. Elements of critical thinking appear in the work of quite a few religious educators. See, for example, Mary Boys, "Access to Traditions and Transformations," in *Tradition and Transformation in Religious Education*, ed. Padraic O'Hare (Birmingham, Ala.: Religious Education Press, 1979), 9–34; Thomas Groome, *Christian Religious Education*; Mary Elizabeth Moore, *Education for Continuity and Change* (Nashville: Abingdon, 1983) and *Teaching from the Heart* (Minneapolis: Fortress, 1991); Linda J. Vogel, *Teaching and Learning in Communities of Faith* (San Francisco: Jossey-Bass, 1991), among others. See also the discussion by Allen J. Moore, "Liberation and the Future of Christian Education," in *Contemporary Approaches to Christian Education*, ed. Jack L. Seymour and Donald E. Miller (Nashville: Abingdon, 1982).

30. The idea of problem-posing education was developed by Paulo Freire, *Pedagogy of the Oppressed* (New York: Seabury, 1973). Much of my thinking about education has been shaped by Freire through his books and personal conversation. See also Jane Vella, *Learning to Listen, Learning to Teach: The Power of Dialogue in Educating Adults* (San Francisco: Jossey-Bass, 1994).

31. See John E. Alsup, "The Role of Listening in Biblical Interpretation," *Austin Seminary Bulletin: Faculty Edition* 92, no. 8 (May 1977): 7–25.

32. The teacher unfamiliar with Bible translations, concordances, and commentaries needs to consult the clergy or denomina-

tional staff for guidance in choosing ones that are considered theologically sound by the denomination.

33. Idea from William Bean Kennedy, "Integrating Personal and Social Ideologies," in Mezirow, *Fostering Critical Reflection in Adulthood* (San Francisco: Jossey-Bass, 1990), 99–115.

34. Linda Shaw Finlay and Valerie Faith, in Mezirow, *Fostering Critical Reflection in Adulthood*, 63–86.

35. Again, Freire is very influential in my thought here; see his discussion of "generative themes" in his *Pedagogy of the Oppressed*, chapter 3.

36. Plaskow, "Jewish Memory from a Feminist Perspective," 47.

37. Ibid.

38. One common definition of ritual is the one used by Edith and Victor Turner: "formal behavior prescribed for occasions not given over to technological routine that have reference to beliefs in mystical beings or powers" (Quoted in *Liturgy Digest* 1, no. 1 [Spring 1993]: 17).

39. See Ronald Grimes, "Liturgical Supinity, Liturgical Erectitude: On the Embodiment of Ritual Authority," in *Studia Liturgica* 23, no. 1 (Spring 1993); and his "Emerging Ritual," in *Proceedings of the North American Academy of Liturgy, Annual Meeting* (St. Louis, Mo., 2–5 January 1990), 15–31. For a helpful summary of these issues, see "Revisiting the Roots of Ritual: Basic Directions in the Field of Ritual Studies," *Liturgy Digest* 1, no. 1 (Spring 1993): 4–36.

40. See "Revisiting the Roots of Ritual," 14–15; also Catherine Bell, "Ritual, Change, and Changing Rituals," *Worship* 63, no. 1 (January 1989).

41. Bell, "Ritual, Change, and Changing Rituals."

42. "What is the chief end of man? Man's chief end is to glorify God and to enjoy him forever." This Westminster Catechism was written in 1647 and was memorized by many generations of Protestant, especially Presbyterian, children. "The Shorter Catechism," *Book of Confessions*, 7.001 (Louisville, Ky.: Presbyterian Church (U.S.A.), 1999).

43. Grimes, "Emerging Ritual," 15–16.

44. See, for example, my article, "Women's Spirituality Empowered by Biblical Story," in *Religious Education* 87, no. 4 (Fall 1992).

45. See Gwen Kennedy Neville and John H. Westerhoff III, *Learning through Liturgy* (New York: Seabury, 1978). Neville's

study of the formal, "inside" ritual systems, run by those in authority, mainly men, and of the more informal, "outside" religious ritual systems, run by women and men with less authority and power, contributes valuable data on religion and ritual.

46. I owe the concept of "talking against the text" to the Rev. Valerie Bridgeman Davis. She describes this act as happening when African American women reinterpret texts that have oppressed them. In her retreats, as well as those led by many clergywomen, the participants then compose new songs, poems, and prayers that express the deeper biblical principles of God's love for and redemption of women.

47. The audiocassette tapes of Colleen Fulmer (*The Cry of Ramah*, 1985, and *Her Wings Unfurled*, 1989, 1990 [Albany, Calif.: Loretto Spirituality Network]) are one example. They come with a booklet in which Martha Ann Kirk describes movements that can be put with the songs.

48. I owe this insight to James A. Sanders's lectures.

Chapter 5: Ten Teaching Tips

1. The pedagogy of Paulo Freire is evident in these statements. See the previous chapter. Note also that children are not blank canvases either, but complex beings who can be treated as active explorers in the learning process.

2. The concept of "making accessible" I owe to Mary Boys, "Access to Traditions and Transformation," in *Tradition and Transformation in Religious Education*, ed. Padraic O'Hare (Birmingham, Ala.: Religious Education Press, 1979), especially 14–15.